PUBLIC AWARENESS

IN

IMPLANT DENTISTRY

How To Double Your Implant Patients In 60 Days Or Less Through Public Awareness

Dr. Joseph A. Gaeta Jr.

Gaeta International

221 Beach Rd. #167

Sarasota, FL 34242

Dedication

To the dental profession, that we come together to create a worldwide outreach dedicated to educating the public about the devastating consequences of tooth loss and the life-changing benefits of dental implants.

To all the seniors I have treated in my twenty-seven years of practice, who have experienced the life-changing benefits of Implant Dentistry.

To Dr. Carl Misch, for his inspiring story about his grandmother in the convalescent home, and the traumatic experiences she expressed as well as her neighbors went through while trying to eat with full dentures.

To Herman, Loretta, and Dave, for their relentless dedication to sharing their stories about how their dental implant experience has literally given them a new lease on life.

To my Dental team, for their daily support OF PERPETUATING THE MESSAGE OF THE DEVISTATING CONSEQUENCES OF BONE LOSS AND THE LIFE CHANGING BENEFITS OF Implant Dentistry.

And lastly, to my Chief Marketing Officer, Lisa, for her relentless drive, dedication, and inspiration from the INCEPTION OF MY VISION, without which the MESSAGE THIS BOOK REVEALS would have never come to fruition.

Foreword

I have been practicing dentistry in southwest Florida for the past twenty-five years. I consider myself blessed to care for seniors, the segment of the population that I consider the "salt of the earth."

In 1993, I had the good fortune to buy a dental practice from Dr. Harold T. Robbins, a crusty old dentist, with a dry sense of humor. He was considered a pioneer in Implant Dentistry and he performed his first dental implant surgery in 1958—the year I was born!

One morning, Dr. Robins came to me and said, "Son, if you want to learn Implant Dentistry and help seniors who can't chew, you better go and get some formal training. If you ever go in front of a judge, you can't tell him the old guy with the gray hair taught you dental implants."

This was the beginning of my education and lifelong mission to educate and treat suffering denture- wearers and people with tooth loss gain a quality of life and be able to chew anything they wanted with confidence, joy, and a smile of satisfaction. This book is dedicated to the dental profession that we may indeed "spread the message" to the entire world about the effects Implant Dentistry can have on people's lives: from facilitating a new loving relationship at 87 years of age, to eliminating embarrassment, to having the confidence to eat any type of food one desires. In short, so that anyone can live the quality of life they deserve!

God Bless,

Dr. Joseph A Gaeta Jr.

Introduction

The world of Implant Dentistry is a rapidly changing one. New advances are being made every day, and the procedures are becoming more affordable for patients every year. Solutions are becoming available that were only dreamed of a few decades ago, and those of us who commit to ongoing education and learning the best and most advanced procedures are at the top of our field.

However, the number of truly life-changing procedures that we do, like placing implants on a ninety year-old female so she can chew and have a better quality of life in her twilight years, is priceles. Reaching the demographic that needs us is vitally important, and we must to reach out to them. We need to educate our seniors about the level of service available to them, and show them we are qualified to do it. We see a massive caseload of patients each year for basic general dentistry, but our hard-earned implant education may not be utilized as much as we would like. Even though we take many surgical and prosthetic courses to learn how to place and restore implants, we rarely learn how to educate our communities about the opportunities available in Implant

Dentistry. We take implant CE courses , get all excited to go back to our practices, then wait for patients to come to us. We may see hundreds of patients a year yet may only either place or restore very few implants during that time.

Does that sound familiar?

I attended the AAID Maxicourse in 1999 ,and the Misch implant Institute (surgical and prosthetic courses in 2000 & 2001), after which during the first year I only placed *five* implants! I ended up with over six-hundred hours of CE in Implant Dentistry with very few implant patients!

"ALL DRESSED UP AND NO WHERE TO GO"

This was not because there are not that many people who need my services, in fact, it is the exact opposite. There were thousands of potential patients out there who both need and could afford implant dentistry. The reason I did not have these patients beating down my practice doors is because I had not reached out to them, I had not focused on educating them, and they didn't know who I was, that I was here, or what I could do for them based on the implant training I had received.

There is a desperate need for the dental profession to create more *public awareness* about the devastating consequences of tooth loss and the life-changing benefits of dental implants. This book is designed to help you, the professional in the dental implant profession identify opportunities to reach out, educate, and make a difference in hundreds of lives in your community every day. You just have to know who needs your help, where and when to share information, and how to get them through your practice's door.

WOULD YOU LIKE TO GENERATE $250,000 FROM NEW IMPLANT PATIENTS?

Do you think it is too good to be true? Well, it is definitely not, and I am going to show you how.

Imagine regularly receiving total case fees of $10,000, $20,000, or even $60,000+ every month while seeing fewer patients that you're seeing now...

Imagine that you are also running a more efficient office *treating fewer patients*, leaving you with more free time for your family, friends, and hobbies.

Best of all, you will be enormously improving the quality of life your patients enjoy!

You can change your life with my positioning strategies because not only will you be seen as the expert in your community but *you will* become the main go-to implant dentist when a patient is considering Implant Dentistry.

Becoming a public awareness expert can help you achieve all of this.

I've been there before,

- Attending over 1,500 hours in postgraduate implant training, taking surgical and prosthetic courses and seeing very few implant patients.
- Going through financial stress at home because of the constant roller coaster of cash flow.
- Enduring sleepless nights thinking about how to get more implant patients through the door.
- Practicing general dentistry just to cover payroll, which actually was taking me further away from what I want to do most—which is to place and restore implants!

You can save time, money, and have all the dental implant cases you want!

For a FREE video training explaining exactly what you need to do visit:

www.publicawarenessacademy.com

Testimonials

"I have witnessed Dr. Gaeta change peoples lives for the past 25 years. Not only do I see complete satisfaction with the patient during and after the implant placement and restorative procedure, but I see Dr. Gaeta's fulfillment of being able to increase the longevity of patients lives by many years. Dental implants have given them the blessing of eating healthy foods that may have not been able to chew prior to having dental implants placed.

Dr. Gaeta's commitment to changing the world and increasing patients knowledge of the devastation of bone loss and the effects it has to human beings is amazing. The passion he shows when he spreads the word of implant dentistry and the positive effects throughout the community is how I will always remember Dr. Gaeta. It has been a learning experience working with Dr. Gaeta and being a part of the dental implant seminars for the past 20 years. I hope to spread the word with him for another 20 years and help him in his passion to create Public Awareness to many more of the worlds population, patients and dental professionals." Kolleen Gaeta, Practice Administrator, Celebrity Smiles Dental, FL

"Our implant seminars have given us the opportunity to take that to a much higher level. I have been the implant seminar *coordinator for several years now and have mastered the process of putting all the tools, staff, materials together to provide an effective presentation to the community. The joy of having people of all back grounds come in searching for answers to ease their suffering and witnessing the hope they receive during our presentation is what I consider DIVINE FULFILLMENT. Assisting a patient whom is a dental cripple from the education process through the implant seminar, the initial in office consultation, to performing and assisting the patient in the surgical procedure, the emotional bonding between the patient, the experience, doctor and team, but most of all the satisfaction and fulfillment of watching the patient go from the inability to eat, smile and function with a sense of social security, to a person whom is now able to live out their best quality of life and enjoy all that it has to offer. I have worked with Dr. Gaeta for 13 years, in the beginning of my career with him, I assisted Dr. Gaeta chairside in all of his implant and surgical procedures. Throughout my career I have transitioned to educating our employees and doctors and leading my co workers in the vision and passion Dr. Gaeta has within him. Dr. Gaeta has a gift of changing peoples lives for the better, this is just one of the many things I have witnessed and patients have communicated to me throughout the years. The blessing I have everyday is the ability to educate my peers and elders on the benefits of implant dentistry." Heather Newcom, Office Manager, Celebrity Smiles Dental, FL*

"My name is Kim and I am a CDA. I have now done 4 Implant seminars with Dr. Gaeta. The best part of the whole experience is educating and meeting our "future" patients. The seminars allow us to introduce ourselves to the community in a casual and relaxed environment. This is very important since most patients have a high fear of coming to the dentist. The seminars are also a chance for our team to get dressed up and step out of the office environment for a day. We always have a great time and I believe our seminar guests do also. I look forward to many more seminars with Dr Gaeta!!!!!" Kimberly Senter, CDA, Celebrity Smiles Dental, FL

"As a clinical assistant, I see firsthand how dental implants change our patients lives, and I enjoy participating in Dr. Gaeta's seminars because of his passion to educate the public about the benefits of dental implants. Implant dentistry truly does change peoples lives. I take pride in assisting patients in their own journey to a healthier, happier lifestyle. The smile on a patient's face cannot be measured by words. It is measured by the light on their face as they can truly enjoy life without restrictions and embarrassment of a denture or a partial. I am blessed to be part of each patient's life changing experience"

Pamela Love Lynch, EFDA, CDA, Celebrity Smiles Dental, FL

"I have been Dr. Gaeta's primary, chair side surgical dental assistant for 14 years. Throughout these years Dr. Gaeta has proven to me how beneficial dental implants are for our patients through my hands on experience assisting him in all of the implant placement procedures we perform, and how dramatically dental implants improve patients lives both physically and emotionally. Implant seminars are such an important component to educating our community to give them the guidance and solutions needed to improve their dental health. Implant dentistry has allowed me to assist Dr. Gaeta in helping others to improve their ability to chew, function and live out their best quality of life."

Dawn Van Wagner,Surgical Dental Assistant, Celebrity Smiles Dental, FL

TABLE OF CONTENTS

CHAPTER 1: THE WORLD IS CHANGING

What is the Principal Contributing Factor to Tooth Loss?

Why Should We Pay Attention to the Baby Boomers?

Why Can Implant Dentists Change the World?

Why is Implant Dentistry Known Today as the New Standard in Dentistry for Tooth Loss?

How is the World Changing for Implant Dentists?

What Direction is Implant Dentistry Moving?

Why Should You Care?

What Can You Do to Bring More Dental Implant Patients through the Door?

What Will Public Awareness Do for You and Your Practice?

CHAPTER 2: THE FUTURE OF IMPLANT DENTISTRY

What Does the Current State of Dentistry Have to Do with the Epidemic of Tooth Loss?

What are the Short-Term Effects of Tooth Loss?

What are the Long-Term Effects of Tooth Loss?

CHAPTER 3: MYTHS AND MISCONSEPTIONS

How is Misinformation a Contributing Factor to Tooth Loss?

Why are the Baby Boomers Important?

Why is it Important to Communicate the Value of Dental Implants?

Why Do We Only Learn about the Nuts and Bolts?

What are the Fantastic Opportunities in the Dental Implant Market Today?

How has the Dental Implant Industry Changed?

CHAPTER 4: THE NEW MARKET

Why is Education-Based Marketing the New Approach?

Why Do We Need a New Approach?

Who Wins, Who Loses?

How Can You Finally Stop Struggling to Get New Implant Patients?

When You Have No Patients You Get Motivated Pretty Quickly

What is the Secret to Finding New Implant Patients?

CHAPTER 5: CREATING A FLOOD OF NEW IMPLANT PATIENTS

How Can I Attract New Implant Patients?

How Can I Reach the People Who Have Tooth Loss?

How Can I Generate Implant Patients Through Public Awareness Seminars?

Others?"

What If "I Do Not Have Time to Implement New Systems in My Practice"?

Why Should 'The Joy Be In The the Journey?

What is the First Thing You Need to Do?

Why Do You Want to Be a Multiple 7-Figure Dentist?

CHAPTER 8: SPREADING THE MESSAGE WORLDWIDE

ENDNOTES

BONUS! Dr. Gaeta's Entire Public Awareness Seminar Transcribed

"Whatever we expect with confidence
becomes our own self-fulfilling
prophecy."
- Brian Tracy

CHAPTER 1

THE WORLD IS CHANGING

What is the Principal Contributing Factor to Tooth Loss?

The problem of tooth loss in adults around the globe is steadily increasing, As human longevity increases, age becomes the most significant contributing factor. Therefore, the opportunity for Implant Dentistry will only increase for years to come.

While the under-45 age bracket can boast that only 2% of their population segment has suffered complete loss of their teeth, by the time they reach the age of 65, 27% of U.S. residents have experienced complete tooth loss and a staggeringly large percentage of the remainder do not even have enough teeth to properly chew. (1)

The minimum number of teeth required for a mouth to be considered functional is 21. The average number of teeth a 65 year-old has left is 18-19, and they lose more teeth every year.(2) The most common solutions of dentures and bridgework often only exacerbate the problem, resulting in even more tooth loss as well as bone loss in the mandible and maxilla.

The numbers worsen exponentially with age: 30-45% of people over the age of 75 in the U.S. have no teeth at all—following a pattern of both tooth loss and bone resorption that increases every year. These edentulous patients are largely ignored by the dental profession and often suffer with ill-fitting dentures and ongoing problems. (3)

Why Should We Pay Attention to the Baby Boomers?

Because treating teeth is "what dentists do," the average dental practice focuses on the under-40 age group, the majority of whom have *not* suffered tooth loss. This leaves a huge portion of the population underserved simply because they are not recognized as a potential patient base.

Most of the attention paid to the geriatric population is geared towards low cost solutions because the prevailing opinion is that seniors do not have the money to spend on their teeth. This erroneous assumption is costing the senior population their teeth, and, by extension, their health, in ever increasing numbers.

For every low-cost stop-gap solution, more teeth are lost; the epidemic worsens, and by age 80, a senior citizen has an almost even chance of having zero teeth left, with many more suffering the ongoing loss of multiple teeth from the upper and lower arches as well as continuous bone loss.

While many seniors can perhaps afford only dentures and bridgework, this is definitely not true for all. There are thousands of people over the age of 65 wearing dentures who *can* afford Implant Dentistry but were never educated about their options. Why? Because of *our* assumption that (a) "seniors have no money," and (b) "seniors do not know about treatment options. This, of course, creates a "just get by" mentality.

I will address both these myths in Chapter 3.

Why Can Implant Dentists Change the World?

Implant dentists can be life-changers for seniors and others who have experienced tooth loss. We can prevent further dentition problems and restore happiness and health to countless patients.

Implant dentistry is about more than cosmetics. It can literally add years to the lives of patients by stopping bone loss and premature aging, increasing bite force and improving diet, and generally increasing quality of life. There are hundreds of implant-trained dentists doing general dentistry because they do not have many patients knocking on their door to inquire about their Implant Dentistry skills.

These patients do exist, though. They just need to be educated about their opportunity to chew again! That is what this book is all about: taking advantage of the endless opportunities available and reaching out to the patients who up to this point have been ignored.

Do you talk to your patients about what happens after they start losing teeth and the consequences that come hard on the heels of tooth loss?.There is a vast, worldwide opportunity to educate and encourage both dental professionals and patients about the silent epidemic of tooth loss, and to improve the standard of care available to patients in need.

As implant dentists, I feel we have a responsibility to reach out and share this information. We have a duty to patients to ensure they have all the information and treatment options for receiving the best standard of care available. We also have a duty to ourselves to put our hard-earned skills and knowledge to use and give our patients the best treatment options and quality of life they deserve.

Why is Implant Dentistry Known Today as the New "Standard Of Care" in Dentistry for Tooth Loss?

The challenge for implant dentists is to properly identify and pursue the many opportunities for Implant Dentistry that already exist, and to present dental implants as an industry best-practice treatment option.

This is not a matter of having to create opportunities—the patients are already out there and in need of our services. Our job is to make sure they are educated about their needs and the consequences of tooth loss and the solutions available to them.

Currently, in the case of patients who have lost the majority of their teeth, partial or full dentures are the primary go-to solution. In the U.S., 80.6% of patients who are edentulous in the lower arch wear a lower denture, 96.8% of patients who are edentulous in the upper arch wear an upper denture, and 89.6% of totally edentulous patients wear full dentures. (4) In my experience, most of these patients would be better served by Implant Dentistry. Even patients who have single tooth loss would benefit much more from a dental implant than a fixed or removable bridge.

Implants have the added benefit of preventing further dental destruction, whereas studies show that within 5 to 7 years, tooth loss adjacent to a removable partial denture or fixed bridgework is 30%. (5)

Educating dentists to educate their patients is the biggest challenge. The end goal is for patients to receive the best possible dental treatment. For edentulous patients, implants are the preferred choice of treatment for edentulous areas of the arch.

To reach this goal, dentists have to be taught how to reach the patients who are both in need of implants and who can afford them. Patients have to be educated about the options available to them as well as the consequences of settling for less than the best treatment option.

How is the World Changing for Implant Dentists?

Rapidly advancing technology has made dental implants easier to place, and new bone graft techniques have made implants a viable treatment option for many patients who previously would not have been considered candidates.

The number of seniors is increasing by the day, and the number of dentists who are trained to perform Implant Dentistry is also increasing. The number of teeth lost annually in the U.S. is around 45 million, according to the American Dental Association, but the number of implants placed annually is barely 2 million. Why? Because the majority of partially or fully edentulous patients are fitted for bridgework or dentures instead of being educated about their options and having their missing teeth replaced with implants.

Many of these patients could have avoided reaching the point of losing most or all of their teeth if given better care initially. However, lack of education leads to stop-gap solutions, particularly where back teeth are involved, causing additional problems over the years.

The most common result of tooth loss is the loss of more teeth. Each tooth helps support and is supported by the teeth on either side of it. Replacing missing teeth with bridgework does nothing to prevent continued bone loss in the pontic/edentulous area. The teeth on either side of the missing tooth take on excess stress and strain, the bone in the socket of the missing tooth begins to resorb, and eventually the adjacent teeth are lost, requiring new bridgework with a longer span, further compromising the abutment teeth.

Bone loss leads to facial changes, including sunken cheeks, sagging skin, and the need to constantly reline or replaced dentures to avoid problems associated with their ill-fitting condition, including pain and denture sores. Dental implants eliminate these problems, yet only a tiny percent of the edentulous population have taken advantage of what is now considered to have the highest success rate in dentistry today: Implant Dentistry.

In the case of one or two teeth lost, or even a half-dozen teeth down the road, many patients may not be offered either all treatment options or the options are not properly explained. This leads to ever increasing dentate destruction.

"THE CONDITION GETS WORSE . . . A CASCADE OF DESTRUCTION CONTINUES"
Dr. Carl Misch

The answer? Start using the best technology to educate all your patients and your community. As life expectancy increases, the number of years the average individual needs a healthy mouth of teeth also increases. Dental implants have become the obvious treatment of choice over this lengthening life span.

What Direction is Implant Dentistry Moving?

Cosmetic Dentistry is a rapidly growing industry, and is likely to remain so barring a significant recession. According to an in-depth study by Straumann (a Switzerland-based dental implant product and services company):

- No substitute for dental implants will emerge in the next 10 years.

- The number of patients with co-morbidities will increase over the same time period.

- Patients will begin to demand more and better information on dental health and treatment options.

- Implant procedures will be driven by prosthetics, increasing productivity and decreasing chair time.

- Investments in new technology will raise the barrier for opening new dental practices.

- Implants will become an increasingly attractive economic option for both dentists and patients.(6)

According to the same study, "Economic pressure in developed countries fosters a 'good enough' mentality among patients and dentists." This is what we need to break away from by educating patients and no longer accepting "good enough" options when the opportunity to provide a higher standard of care is available—one that can give the real people we care for the best possible quality of life.

Why Should You Care?

I am full blooded Italian—third-generation Sicilian. I grew up in Omaha, Nebraska, working in my parents' restaurant. Starting at the age of six, I began by standing on a milk crate in front of the broiler waiting for an order of garlic bread to come in. I credit my experiences in the restaurant business for teaching me the value of hard work, multi-tasking, improving manual dexterity, and for the attitude of helping and serving others. The eye-hand coordination I gained and the great attitude towards hard work and service to others has stood the test of time. It has proven invaluable in my chosen career, which now includes 23 solid years of placing and restoring dental implants. I also have performed IV parenteral conscious sedation for 25 years.

I graduated from Creighton University, School of Dental Science, in Omaha, Nebraska in 1986. In 1988 I moved to Sarasota, Florida to open my own practice. Through the years, I have logged over 1,500 hours in post-graduate dental implant education, and in 2000 I achieved Board Certification status with the American Board of Oral Implantology / Implant Dentistry (ABOI/ID), joining the fewer than 500 dentists worldwide who have achieved such status.

I trained for both surgical and restorative specialties, meaning I not only place the implants but also restore them to function, which very few dentists in the U.S. can claim. I am also certified in IV parenteral conscious sedation, which enables me to perform extended treatment plans with the patient experiencing little or no anxiety or remembering any of the procedure at all.(1o appoints in1.com)

All of this specialty training took years. I kept telling myself it would be worth it. I went to school, took continuing education courses in Implant Dentistry, learned all the clinical skills needed to accomplish everything about sinus lifts, chin grafts, placing and restoring implants. I was going to be *the* destination for dental implant patients, the "one-stop shop" for restorative dentistry. I was going to have the knowledge and training (enough tools in my tool box) so when a patient came in to the office "hating their dentures", I would have the skill sets to provide ALL treatment to give them an implant supported fixed dentition or an implanted supported over denture.

However, when patients failed to show up at the door of my practice I felt like I was "all dressed up with no place to go." I had invested $75,000+ in implant training, I had less than 500 ABOI/ID competitors practicing at my skill level around the globe, but I was sitting in my office using hardly any of it. I had all the skills, all the shiny new technology, but no implant patients. Where did I go wrong?

However much I had learned about Implant Dentistry, I had not learned how to market my skills and educate my community. I knew the patients needing my services were out there, but I did not know how to reach them. There was simply no continuing education for implant dentists about marketing and creating public awareness for themselves.

I looked for information on how to market myself and create public awareness, but traditional sales techniques were not specific enough to my industry. I started doing my own research and slowly learned who my best patients were, where they were, what they needed, and what they wanted.

I also discovered that I did not have to sell my skill and expertise: Implant Dentistry sold itself once people knew it was available and understood what dental implants could do to improve the quality of their lives. The education itself moved them closer to accepting treatment.

At first the program was just my personal method of raising awareness and getting patients into my practice. Eventually, however, I realized that the principles and strategies that were working for me would work for others in my field just as well, and I decided to create a coaching and consulting program to help implant dentists position themselves through public awareness as the perceived implant expert in their communities. That is how the Public Awareness Academy was born.

"They may forget what you said, but they will never forget how you made them feel."
- Carl Buechner

What Can You Do to Bring More Dental Implant Patients through the Door?

Following the suggestions in this book can change your life! Imagine just one new implant patient per week—that is $4,000 per week x 48 weeks = $192,000 per year—and just by introducing a new thought pattern into the profession about creating public awareness! Instead of having 95% of your practice being general dentistry, you will finally to do more implants and help serve others the way you always intended, instead of just, as we say, "drill, fill and bill."

What Will Public Awareness Do for Your Practice?

This book contains a step-by-step process that will teach you:

- Why you have not yet been able to reach more patients..

- How to position yourself as *the authority* in your community in the field of Implant Dentistry.

- What you need to do to promote yourself and your practice effectively.

- Who your target demographic is and how to reach them.

- Where your priorities should be moving forward.

- When to get started (hint: it is spelled *n-o-w*).

It is time for change. You can stop just practicing General Dentistry and become a life-changing part of your community by educating people about the devastating consequences of tooth loss and the life-changing benefits of Implant Dentistry.

"The way we communicate with others and with ourselves ultimately determines the quality of our lives."
- Anthony Robbins

Chapter 2

THE FUTURE OF IMPLANT DENTISTRY

What is the Current State of Dentistry Have to Do with the Epidemic of Tooth Loss?

Tooth loss is becoming an ever increasing concern among Americans, particularly the age 65 and over demographic. In the 1950s, community water sources were not fluoridated and life expectancy was only 68 years. (7) Thanks to technological and medical advances, those who are 65 today have another decade or so of life expectancy instead of just three more years. However, their teeth are not lasting as long, and this can actually decrease life expectancy as well as quality of life.

Gum disease and tooth decay are the main reasons for initial tooth loss, but the greatest reasons for subsequent tooth loss are lack of support from previously lost teeth and deterioration of bone holding the teeth in place.

Once a single tooth is lost, the ones on either side may quickly follow. A bridge or partial dentures can provide a solid chewing surface, but these options do not support the remaining teeth and may even contribute to their loss as extra strain is added by using them to support the bridgework.

Eventually, so many teeth are lost that facial structure changes (the premature aging-look phenomenon), eating becomes a chore (decrease in bite force), and other issues loom as overall health deteriorates. This silent epidemic of tooth and bone loss starts taking prisoners who often do not know where to turn or how to get help.

What can we, as dentists, do to alleviate the problems caused by tooth loss? First is to recognize that teeth are not our primary concern, rather, we must assess the entire needs of the body. As mentioned earlier in this book, edentulous patients are far to often overlooked by the dental community because "dentists treat teeth." When we stop treating teeth and treat the entire patient instead, things change.

The technical nature of the dental profession is responsible for the years we spend learning procedures and proper instrumentation. In dental school, though, we are offered only a minimal orientation to patient education through public awareness.

Our goal should always be to present the best

treatment option for our patients, and in order to provide this care we have to be able to educate our communities about the dangers of tooth loss and the consequences that follow when proper steps are not taken to prevent more damage.

What are the Short-Term Effects of Tooth Loss?

The immediate effects of tooth loss are relatively insignificant. Once a tooth is completely lost or extracted and any pain or infection is dealt with, the effects on daily life are primarily cosmetic—with incisors or canines being the most apt to prompt quick action, while back molars are often ignored.

Discomfort or inconvenience when eating is the next most common effect, and is often mitigated by chewing on the opposite side of the mouth. A stop-gap solution like a bridge is often the fastest, cheapest way to "fix" the issue of a lost tooth, but this does nothing to prevent the long term effects of tooth loss and bone loss from continuing.

What are the Long-Term Effects of Tooth Loss?

The long-term effects of tooth loss are much more severe. Bone loss begins immediately after tooth loss, and the teeth on either side of the missing tooth have to take on additional strain from chewing and from any bridgework anchored to them.

This leads to additional tooth loss, which in turn can cause changes to facial structure (premature aging). Patients who are partially or fully edentulous are more likely to develop social issues due to feeling embarrassed or ashamed about their appearance. Chewing becomes increasingly difficult due to continued bone loss, and eating healthy foods gets progressively more difficult. This cascade of destruction can contribute in turn to obesity, diabetes, and other health-related problems caused or contributed to by bad nutrition.

CHAPTER 3

MYTHS AND MISCONSEPTIONS

How is Misinformation a Contributing Factor to Tooth Loss?

In many cases, patients are misinformed about their choices. This is especially true of younger people with little or no insurance, who simply want to get the "problem" fixed as quickly and as inexpensively as possible. They are given the services they ask for and sent on their way without knowing the long-term effects of their tooth loss.

For older patients with multiple missing teeth, extensive bridgework and partial dentures is the usual treatment option; while for patients who are completely edentulous in one or both arches, the go-to solution is complete dentures. A common concern is that patients never become educated on the consequences of long term tooth loss.

Failure to properly support remaining teeth leads inexorably to their loss, which is a sad state of affairs considering how easy it is to stop tooth loss and retain natural teeth (as well as bone, facial structure, and normal eating habits) through Implant Dentistry.

How can we stop the cycle of tooth loss? The first step is discarding some of the myths we ourselves hold onto concerning our largest patient demographic.

What are the Myths Surrounding Dental Care for Seniors?

While there are plenty of young people who have experienced tooth loss through trauma or accident, the main demographic not being reached by the dental implant industry is seniors. Sadly, several myths stand in the way of providing cutting edge services to this population.

- Myth A: Seniors cannot afford the best dental care available.

- Myth B: Seniors do not care about the appearance of their teeth.

We all know about the struggles facing seniors in the U.S. We have heard the horror stories about how choices have to be made between groceries and prescriptions, about dreary retirement homes and summer heat stroke from lack of air conditioning. However, not all seniors are struggling to make ends meet on a minimal check from Social Security.

In fact, there is a huge subset of the population that just over the past two years has begun reaching senior status. A significant number of these individuals planned ahead for retirement, managed to dodge the real estate and stock market slumps of the past few years, and are motivated and able to pay for top-of-the-line dental care.

Why are the Baby Boomers Important?

There are 76.4 million people in the U.S. known as "baby boomers". Since January 1, 2011, these individuals started reaching the age of 65. They continue to move over into "senior territory" at the rate of around 10,000 a day. (8) That is over 3,600,000 people who reached retirement age in 2012 alone.

As mentioned, over a quarter of these 65 year olds have no teeth at all, and the majority do not have enough teeth to be considered "functional". Many are already wearing partial or full dentures, and most are deeply unhappy with their smile.

While many seniors do struggle financially and will always opt for the lowest cost level of care, many of the baby boomers do have the means to afford the best in dental care. Around 20% of baby boomers have assets which are projected to total $200,000 or more by 2015, and income over $50,000 per year. This includes 1,440,000 well-to-do seniors aged 65-66 as of January 1, 2013, and an additional 2,000 more in this income bracket will be turning 65 every single day. (9) That is a lot of potential patients—and a debunking of "Myth A".

These seniors are not struggling on Social Security and forced to take the simplest, cheapest option offered. They are financially stable and able to afford higher quality, longer lasting dental reconstruction. They are also more likely to demand better overall health to maintain their lifestyles, including the ability to eat and enjoy their favorite foods and stay fit for activities such as golfing, dancing, and travel.

These individuals also care deeply about the

appearance of their teeth. In several recent studies, dental work was the leading cosmetic change desired by seniors. In a poll of 1,018 adults 18 and over, 80% stated they would have cosmetic work done to alleviate the appearance of aging. Of that group, 62% said they would opt for dental work over weight loss.

Of those polled, 45% said that a great smile was the top age defying trait (compared to a person's eyes, body shape, hair and legs). Of those in the over-50 age group, that percentage jumped to 54%. (10) Obviously, these respondents care about how their teeth look—and that is "Myth B" debunked.

The top 20% of baby boomers definitely *do* care about the appearance of their teeth and are financially able to afford superior care. These people present a golden opportunity for the dental industry. Our job is to provide education, care, and long-lasting solutions to both improve their overall health and prevent additional loss of teeth and bone.

With less than 500 board-certified professionals qualified to place dental implants, there is no reason for every single one of us not to be performing Implant Dentistry exclusively. The patient base is more than large enough to support our practices. We just have to learn how to reach the correct patient demographic.

Why is It Important to Communicate the Value of Dental Implants?

We can start the education process by learning how to communicate the value of dental implants. Currently, the dental industry is all too quick to present options to patients in a technical, feature-driven manner, but it has been proven that patients respond more positively to benefit-driven presentations.

Dentists should learn to communicate the benefits of dental implants to their patients in simple, clear, and easy to understand ways. The focus should be on the day-to-day advantages of implants over dentures or bridgework rather than the technical features of the restoration procedure. Always emphasize how a person will feel: no embarrassment, no loose teeth, increased self-esteem.

First, start mentioning dental implants as an

option during your consultations. This seems like a no-brainer, but it is amazing how often the dental implant option is not even presented to patients at all. Once the option is on the table, the opportunity to discuss the health and social benefits comes in. We will cover these later, but at the same time you cover the cost, health, and social benefits that dental implants offer, you should be prepared to provide information on how implants can improve appearance and reduce the chances of further tooth and bone loss.

Why Do We Only Learn about the Nuts and Bolts?

Sadly, the current public perception of dental implants is either non-existent (they do not know about them as a treatment option) or they think dental implants are too expensive. We need to come together, as colleagues and as a profession, to bring awareness about the benefits of Implant Dentistry to the world, as well as to our own patient base.

Dental implants are primarily marketed from a cosmetic angle, with the health benefits being completely overlooked or ignored. This makes implants look like an unnecessary luxury instead of a very needed and practical treatment option.

My "legacy vision" is to create worldwide awareness about the benefits of dental implants. Go to www.WDIAO.com (World Dental Implant Awareness Organization) and become a member and contribute to creating worldwide awareness.

It is our obligation as health care providers to provide the best possible care for each of our patients. The first step in this process is to create awareness about the benefits of dental implants and provide information about how they can help to increase the overall quality of life.

What are the Fantastic Opportunities in the Dental Implant Market Today?

There is an implant organization called ABOI/ID (American Board of Oral Implantology/Implant Dentistry). The following description is taken directly from their website: *The American Board of Oral*

Implantology / Implant Dentistry was chartered in 1969 by the American Academy of Implant Dentistry (AAID). The Board's mission is to elevate the standards and advance the science and art of Oral Implantology/Implant Dentistry by encouraging its study and improving its practice.

The ABOI/ID Diplomat designation symbolizes the highest level of competence in Implant Dentistry. Certification by the ABOI/ID attests to the fact that a dentist has demonstrated knowledge, ability, and proficiency in Implant Dentistry through a rigorous examination process. There are approximately 500 implant dentists who have achieved such status. The International Congress of Oral Implantologists (ICOI), as well as others, also offers diplomat status. The Misch Implant Institute offers surgical & prosthetic courses with a certification process to obtain a "Diplomat" status.

Implant dentists need the proper training. I recommend you get it. I attended the AAID Maxicourse and went through the Misch Implant Institute, receiving their diplomat status. I am also an associate fellow of the AAID and a diplomat of the ICOI.

I use my diplomat status as a positioning strategy in answering the question "Why should I go to YOU for my implant treatment when I can go to the dentist down the street?"

Again, with over 30 million Americans living without teeth, and with an ever increasing number of these Americans having the means and the motivation to accept dental implant treatment, there are enough patients for every one of us to run a full-time practice doing nothing but Implant Dentistry.

I have been practicing for 27 years, placing and restoring implants for over 23 of them. I have experienced a tremendous amount of personal satisfaction seeing the joy on patients' faces when they say to me, "I can chew again!" There is nothing more satisfying... Having repeatedly witnessed the transformation of patients' entire personas, I felt It was my *mission* to create awareness of such potential in my community and teach other implant dentists worldwide to do the same.

Implant Dentistry is expected to expand by at least 10% in 2014, thanks to the changes listed in the following section. We live in a very exciting and opportune time!

How has the Dental Implant Industry Changed?

Many great changes have occurred in the dental industry over the past few decades. These changes have made implants a better option than ever before for tooth replacement. The good news:

- Dental implants have been consistently improving in quality and ease of placement. Twenty-five years ago, each procedure was grueling and took 6-9 months and multiple visits to a specialist to complete. Today the process is much more rapid and the patient's downtime and discomfort have been significantly lessened.

- The patient demographic has broadened. Baby boomers are rejecting dentures and bridgework and looking for long lasting, attractive, healthy solutions.

- Cosmetic Dentistry has become mainstream. Implants are an integral part of the Cosmetic Dentistry revolution. More and more patients who become partially or fully edentulous will have to consider implant treatment.

- Dental implants have an ever increasing success rate—up to 95% or higher over 10 years. This is significantly higher than many other traditional services, including root canal therapy, crowns, bridges, and removable dentures.

- Implants are slowly becoming recognized as the treatment of choice for patients with tooth loss, and implant treatment has become part of the core curriculum at most dental schools.

- More patients are now considered viable candidates for implants, thanks to advancements in implant designs and bone grafting procedures. Even patients with significant bone loss can now have predictable implant treatment.

- Insurance coverage is slowly starting to catch on. More and more dental insurance companies are covering some of the cost of implant treatment—mostly because it cuts down on their reimbursements in the long run. An implant with a crown costs roughly the same as a three-unit bridge, but statistically the implant lasts longer and over time cost less to the patient while prolonging the life of the teeth adjacent to the edentulous area.(11)

Overall, implants are the better choice for both partially and fully edentulous patients; they are becoming the standard-of-care treatment option. Smiling and chewing are basic patient desires, and numerous other benefits accompany dental implants.

The bad news is that patients are not being informed enough about this option, and many dentists do not even bring up implants when presented with a patient who has suffered tooth loss. Patients never find out that opting for bridges or dentures can severely damage their health, causing additional tooth loss, bone loss, and even more severe conditions later in life.

For example, edentulous denture patients who only see their dentist for new dentures every 14-15 years do not realize they are constantly losing bone over that time period and that they are facing issues like severe facial distortion. It is like a diabetic who has not been diagnosed and then faces blindness or foot amputation because no one told him or her what was happening to the body.

The same goes for patients who opt to have bridgework done to rectify missing teeth and who do not know that they have a 30% chance of losing the teeth on either side of the gap within five to seven years. (12) The "premature aging phenomena" (wrinkling skin, chin closer to the nose), continuous bone loss and other issues could be completely prevented simply by choosing dental implants as the best option to stop bone loss, stabilize arch width, maintain existing dentition, and restore the dentition to full function, form, and health.

We need to educate our communities about the consequences of tooth loss and empower them to do something about it with Implant Dentistry. We, as dentists, need to create more awareness. A whole new approach is needed to ensure that patients are fully informed of their options and of the short- and long-term consequences of loosing teeth.

"Commitment in the face of conflict produces character."
- Mark Twain

CHAPTER 4

THE NEW
MARKET

Why is Education-Based Marketing the New Approach?

Educating people creates opportunities for your practice. Whether you are reaching out to general dentists in your area or mounting a campaign to take the information directly to the patients themselves, the important thing is to focus on spreading educational information instead of presenting a sales pitch. Patients need to know the "why" behind your implant recommendation.

I've been educating people for years, and now I want to teach others in my field to do the same. If every one of us works in our community to reach out and inform people about the consequences of tooth loss and the benefits of dental implants, we can literally save lives that would otherwise be cut short due to problems arising from tooth loss.

I have proven to myself over and over again that if I simply provide information, people get excited and start asking questions—which allows me to share yet more information. If I talk to them about their needs, they always want to know more.

We live in an era that gives us dozens of great

ways to disseminate information both to potential patients and among colleagues. We can distribute information online via websites, videos, webinars, social media, and more, and keep the information flowing offline as well.

Why Do We Need a New Approach?

Right now, information about dental implants is presented as a luxury cosmetic an "if-you-have-the-money" option. While appearances are important to our patients, this type of preconception—that implants are only for the wealthy and are primarily for restoring the look of a smile—prevents us from reaching our broadest demographic. We often sell smiles rather than serve our patients' health needs.

When I saw this failure to address the very real needs and concerns of dental patients, I realized we needed a new way of creating public awareness about dental implants. We needed new ways of learning, new ways of educating, new ways of reaching out and communicating with patients.

Who Wins, Who Loses?

Once you start educating patients about the health benefits of dental implants and about the differences in long-term health and happiness made by implants compared to bridgework or dentures, you will see a significant number of them opting for the better procedure to replace their missing teeth. That means you win, they win, and their loved ones win.

Who loses? Both the dentists who do not take advantage of the incredible opportunities in front of them and their patients—whom they did not inform.

To win, all you have to do is learn the new techniques I outline further on in this book so you can pass this knowledge on to your patients. Believe me, your practice will expand, and you will be able to start using those skills you sacrificed so much time and effort to acquire. *You will feel more fulfilled and the monetary gain will be significant!*

* * * * *

Discover the exact system I use to educate my community so that they perceive me as the obvious expert. Go to:
www.publicawarenessacademy.com

* * * * *

How Can You Finally Stop Struggling to Get Patients?

As I mentioned earlier, I struggled for years trying to figure out what I was doing wrong. I had worked so hard to educate myself and spent years on implant continuing education. I had a great practice, all of the latest technology, all of the passion you can imagine, but the patients I hoped would flock to my door failed to show up.

I started looking for the reasons behind the apparent lack of dental implant prospects, and discovered several things:

- Dentists were still using dentures and bridges as the standard of care.

- Patients often had no idea that implants were an option for them.

- Patients were assuming that implants were too expensive.

- Patients were scared of the procedure (too painful), and did not understand it.

- Patients did not understand what dentures or a bridge meant to their future health.

- Patients did not know about the devastating long term consequences of tooth loss such as decrease bite force, premature aging appearance, continued bone loss, and decrease in life expectancy.

The problem was not a lack of potential patients—they were out there, all right. The problem was a lack of *information*. That is when I realized that the only way I was going to reach these potential patients was to find out where they went for information, and provide it to them.

It worked! Over the years I developed a system for reaching communities and providing education and information about dental implants and the rising epidemic of tooth loss as "the silent aging process" that plagues our senior citizens.

I gathered testimonials from patients who had undergone Implant treatment and helped them share their stories. I gave them a place to talk about how much less frightening getting implants was than they had expected. They had inspiring stories of how much their lives changed by having a healthy mouth of teeth again. I started an awareness campaign and wrote the book *How Your Missing Teeth Are*

Killing You about the epidemic of tooth loss in the U.S. I quickly experienced a significant increase in new implant patients. They came through my doors knowing exactly what they wanted and why.

When You Have No Patients You Get Motivated Pretty Quickly

I got motivated very quickly early on in my dental career and had many sleepless nights trying to figure out how to generate more revenue to pay back the money I had spent on implant training. I wanted to figure out how to do what I loved—placing and restoring dental implants.

In 1986 I became an associate of Dr. Jim Demman. Dr. Demman was placing and restoring subperiosteal implants as well as well as performing IV conscious sedation. He used to say to me, "sell the sizzle," that is, talk about the *benefits* of dental treatment, not the features!

Dr Demman had a regular visitor, a friend who owned seven McDonald's. They always talked about how McDonald's marketed the "sizzle": baseball, apple pie, and McDonalds—not the nutritional benefits. He said that there were only three reasons why people did not go to the dentist: number one was fear; number two was money; number three was low dental IQ.

Dr Demman himself started in the early 70s owning five denture centers. His phone number was 39–smile! He sold those five practices and bought a private practice and I was his first associate.

He heavily marketed dentures by placing a very large ad in the newspaper. He said that for every 10 reline patients you would get a new denture patient, and for every 10 denture patients you would get an implant patient. He was good at tracking his statistics and was always very close to that average.

I saw that the more he got his name out there into the community the more implant consults came his way. He said that it is basic behavioral psychology: the more times you see something the closer you get to a response. For example, a direct mail piece might have an average of a 2% response rate if delivered only one time to a household. But studies have shown that after the seventh time the direct-mail piece went out, the response rate soared to up to 80%!

He told me that if you got your name out there you would be perceived as an expert. With humility, he said that his clinical skills may not be as good as another dentist but he was still considered an expert because of all the public awareness he created in the community.

After all my clinical training, though, catching on to even such simple marketing was not easy. I was just like every other new implant dentist, I bet. Just like you, I would go to a seminar, come back all fired up and ready to go, only to then face office and clinical staff who did not understand why I was so enthusiastic! Finally I realized I needed to educate my own staff about Implant Dentistry.

From then on, after I came back from attending an implant seminar I would have an hour-and-a-half staff meeting where I would explain to everyone what I'd learned, including the "keeping-it-simple" key phrases and significant statistics that they were required to memorize. I actually had pop quizzes! Or I told them that we would be having a test on this material next week! You can imagine the look on their faces! During the week I would quiz them on what they had learned, like how much bite force did a denture have compared to natural teeth?

My "Ah-ha" dream.

I woke up one night at 2 a.m. from a dream in which I understood the "one-to-many strategy." That is, if I held a public seminar about Implant Dentistry I could fill a room with potential implant patients. They could get to know me and I could build trust and confidence with them. I also could invite my implant patients whose treatments were finished to attend and they could share their personal stories about their experience with their implants. I could do a PowerPoint presentation talking about the history of Implant Dentistry, the consequences of tooth loss, the different treatment options using dental implants, and cover other frequently asked questions.

I would have staff in the back of the room making no-charge consultations after the seminar. I could also stay after the seminar to answer any other questions anyone might have. I would also be available to personally sign their copy of my book.

THE SEMINAR WAS A SUCCESS!

At my first seminar, over ten years ago, I scheduled more than $42,000 in Implant Dentistry!

At my last implant seminar, of 62 people who called for information, 42 attended the seminar, 15 scheduled complimentary consultations, and 8 scheduled for implant treatment—a total of $87,000 in implant and restorative dentistry! That was only 8 out of the 62 who called to inquire about the seminar. The remaining potential implant patients receive timely educational implant information so that when they are ready for treatment I am the implant dentist they call first. This is called a TOMA Campaign: Top of Mind Awareness.

TOMA means that these potential patients are thinking of *you*, and come to *you first*.

Taking into account that studies show we forget approximately 80% of what we've learned after two weeks, and that currently in our society (according to marketing studies) we get exposed to something like 3,700 forms of distraction each day in the form of marketing and advertizing campaigns of all sorts, with my success rate I realized I had found the solution!

Public Awareness Seminars are the quickest

way to generate implant business. I love doing large treatment plans the most: sedate the patient, placing them in a very relaxed/amnesic state and placing implants. This often generates about $10,000 for the two hours of work.

My favorite scenario is when a patient with a full upper and lower dentures comes in complaining that the lower denture is loose. The treatment plan is IV sedation, three to four implants in the lower anterior mandible with the Hadar bar and new upper and lower dentures for $10,000 discounted from $15,000!

Two of these cases per week creates $80,000 per month in new revenue! Let's say you work 38 weeks per year taking two weeks off. That gives you an extra $760,000 in income from just two more implant patients per week. And as an implant dentist, lower anterior mandible, three to four implants with a Hadar bar or locators is one of the easiest and most lucrative treatments available to all suffering denture wearers.

What is the Secret to Finding New Implant Patients?

The secret to finding an abundance of people to serve in your community is really no secret at all. It is not some fancy marketing scheme or advertising tactic. It is about strategically positioning yourself as an expert in your community through PUBLIC AWARENESS. Now, I realize that your media reps will not show up on your doorstep proclaiming such a bland sales pitch, but that is really the key when it comes to finding people in your community who are perfect candidates for dental implants.

When you want to reach a specific potential patient for a large dental implant case, how are you certain they even know they need implants? What if they have no idea that the missing teeth in their mouth can cause significant consequences? Where would they have learned that? I have found that traditional print advertising may not the best way to bring new patients through the door.

What about the demographics of seniors, who make up the main segment of the population needing dental implants? Many of them enjoy reading newspapers and magazines. It would be foolish for me to suggest that you not advertise in the newspaper if that is one of the best ways to reach them.

The reason why I consistently have $14,000-$20,000 days in my practice is because I focus most of my advertising/marketing efforts on public awareness. I sincerely care about the well-being of my community and take the time to educate the people in it. In doing so, I help them learn things they never knew about their teeth. I get them to know, like, and trust me. I not only build rapport with my community but also open the doors to let me help them.

In 1993 I decided to do my first public seminar about the benefits of dental implants. I have to tell you, I never took a speech class in college because I did not want to get up in front of anybody! Just the thought of standing in front of people made me nervous, but I knew people needed to be educated. *We* have to educate them about what happens when *they* lose a tooth! What happens when they lose all their teeth? They do not know what happens and they do not know why it happens and they do not know any of the consequences when it happens. The only way for me to educate my community was to put on a public seminar and tell them.

I first had to find a location. Having been brought up in the restaurant business, I figured a similar venue would be good. I found a cultural center close to my office. It had an open room that could be setup classroom-style. I ran a series of black-and-white ads in the local newspaper offering a complimentary continental breakfast and a free gift for coming. I was so nervous. I had two staff members setup in the back of the room and stand ready to make appointments after the seminar. I had another one greeting at the door.

As each person walked in I could feel myself starting to get more and more nervous. After I introduced myself and had launched into the PowerPoint presentation, I realized that I was authentic enough, even with all my slipups. It was clear that the attendees were drawn to the education I was giving them and many asked questions; some even told of their personal struggles. At the end, I offered complimentary consultations at my office, and, to my delight, many lined up in the back of the room to make an appointment for later that day.

Most of the people who attended had no prior knowledge of the consequences of tooth loss. All it took was for me to take the time to inform them and for them to get to trust me. In the end, I ended up closing multiple implant cases. I was ecstatic! I had created a system for generating new implants patients and could start using the knowledge I learned from my 1,500+ hours in post graduate implant education!

Over the years I have refined my Public Awareness Seminar system. In fact, on average, I now generate at least $100,000 in new implant business from every seminar I put on. The system has been refined, yet its sole purpose as an educational seminar remains the same. If you focus on education rather than selling you build trust and close many more implant cases. I have "positioned" myself in my area with my Public Awareness Seminars; in fact, some of my patients love coming to the seminar to share their implant treatment experience!

Three in particular: Herman, Loretta and Dave, have become like family to me. I call them my "roadies," because no matter where I hold a dental implant seminar they always come. Herman is now 91 years old! He has implant-supported fixed bridge work upper and lower. Loretta had upper and lower partials; she now has implant-supported fixed. Dave has upper and lower implant-supported over dentures.

They welcome the opportunity to stand up and hold the microphone and tell their story of success.

Here is a transcript from one of my recent dental implant seminars where Herman, Loretta, and Dave tell their success stories to the audience.

Dr. Gaeta: This is, Herman, who is my surrogate father. He's become a friend and he actually had an upper denture that he doesn't have anymore. He has all fixed teeth. So Herman, do you want to go ahead and tell a little about your experience?

Herman: Sure, I'll be glad to.

One of the best decisions I made in my life, and I made a lot of good ones and a lot of bad ones, was to have implants put into my mouth. The frosting on the cake was I had Dr. Gaeta and his staff do the job. It doesn't matter how long it takes. I had false teeth and I hated them. Most of the time, they were in my pocket. I absolutely hated them. I'd go into restaurants and I would eat with the paper in front of me and do all sorts of crazy things. I'd been looking for implants for years.

I probably got a call from Joe

around 10 years ago. There are a lot of pluses. For me, the first time it took a year to do the whole thing. In that process though, I learned a lot about Dr. Gaeta and his staff. I realized that he was dedicated to his profession and he enjoyed his work, which is a big plus. He built a staff around him who were compassionate and caring, so it's been a good experience.

Another plus is that the very first time I went in there, he put me to sleep. He took my false teeth, threw them away and made some temporary teeth. The temporaries were really in a sense almost as good as the permanent ones that I have now. It took a year. First, he put some cow bone in there. I was running around saying moo moo. That's what they do to you. Then it took four or five months for that to get all hooked up and stuffed it up.

In the process, I would see Joe and I think I'm part of the family now. I gained a friend with the staff and good Joe. I enjoy coming to see Joe and his staff, even if I'm not going to have any work done. It's been a plus from the very beginning.

Anyhow, after the four months, then he put the implants in and I got a kick out of him. He put them in there and he torqued them. I thought what the heck, are we putting wheels on cars? Whoever heard of getting your teeth torqued? I learned a lot of good things. I recommend that if you're thinking about having anything done, talk with Joe. Go in, see him and think about it. I guarantee it, you will never be sorry that you did and that you picked him and his staff. I'm happy and I'm glad. Like I said, I've become like family and that's a real plus in this world. Thank you.

Dr. Gaeta: The next gentleman is Dave who has a lower denture. I put some dental implants in on the lower denture and with a bar Dave snaps in his teeth. Dave, do you want to talk more about your experience?

Dave: I'm relatively new at this because I only had this done just about two years ago now. My experience with Dr. Gaeta was--this is going to sound funny coming from a patient going to see a dentist—wonderful. A pure pleasure because I had no pain and no discomfort whatsoever afterwards. The process was smooth and like Herman, with the extensive work that I had to have done, it took about a year.

Since I've had it done, I can eat

anything I want from steak, peanuts and cashews to apples. I'm not worried about my dentures falling out and embarrassing me if my wife and I are out to dinner.

If you can't eat and chew properly, you don't have good health. If you don't have good health, you don't have anything at all. Being able to eat anything that I want, when I want and knowing that it's doing me good and that my health's good and what it cost me to have the work done was well worth it. In my estimation, you cannot put a price on good health. Like I said before, without it you have nothing.

[Applause]

Dr. Gaeta: Thank you, Dave. Now I'd like to introduce you to Loretta Cooper. Loretta's like a surrogate mother to me and she knows if I'm working too hard in the office, she'll tell me. We were talking earlier, it's like she'll grab my ear through the phone when I talk to her. Loretta had partials. She had partial plates that she took in and out. Now she doesn't have partials anymore. We did some implants on Loretta. Loretta, would you like to tell them about your experience, please?

Loretta: *Sure. Thank you.*

I always like to say its Herman's fault that I'm here, because I watched him go through everything. He's a family friend and I watched him going through the dental implant because I hate dentists. I say it quietly, but I really did. I had terrible experiences as a young person and stayed away from dentists, unfortunately, for a lot of years.

I had a lot of damage by the time I saw Dr. Gaeta. I had the partial plates. I had them made when I lived in Pennsylvania. When I came to see Dr. Gaeta, he told me I would leave there that day with teeth in my mouth once he did some of the implants. I was very embarrassed because first, my teeth were being damaged by the plates that I had and I knew that they were wearing out.

I was embarrassed because when I went to a restaurant, I'd always have to get up, walk away, say excuse me, go into the ladies room and take the dentures out to rinse them and then put them back in because food particles would get underneath and they would make my mouth very sore.

Dr. Gaeta promised me I wouldn't have that

anymore. Like I said, I was petrified and the staff knew I was petrified. They used to literally hold my hand. Dr. Gaeta's brother-in-law isn't here today, that's Mike, but he and I are two of the biggest cowards you'd ever see. When I go into Joe and he's going to work on my mouth, he'll make sure I'm very comfortable.

I have work that he's doing now. I had to stop it because I had some surgery and I have two more implants going on, on this side and God knows what he's going to do over here. I just let him do it now. He tells me what I need and I go okay. Put me to sleep and I don't care what you do. When he puts me to sleep, I really don't care what he does because when I wake up, I'm fine.

Do I have a lot of pain? No. I had been given pain medication. I'm super-sensitive to medications and Joe knows that. The first time he had given me pain medication I couldn't take it and I actually ended up taking Motrin, which was all I needed to get me through was the Motrin. I had one day of uncomfortable-ness, whereas by the next day, the pain was gone.

I walked out of that office. I also had a partial

on this side with a tooth, which he took and did away with. I still have bridge work. He's working on that. I was very conscious of my smile. I wouldn't smile. I really was very conscious of my smile because of the clasp and I was afraid of food being there.

He took my partials that day and threw them in the trash and I was like, wow. I came out of there with a temporary and like Herman said the temporaries were just as good. Herman talked about the staff. I can't say enough about the staff. They have been so – they become your children. At my age, they're my children and they really are compassionate. They really care about you. They stayed by me when I got sick one time.

When I'm not there, they pick up the phone and they call to see if I'm okay. So when Herman said it becomes like a family, it really does. The first thing I asked for today was where is Josephine and Joe, because I didn't see them. I didn't know where they were, and they're here today. It was so neat to see them. I'll just say that if you're interested in changing your life – I couldn't eat right either.

If you're interested in changing your life and your smile, I suggest – for me, it wasn't just *the smile. It was the eating, which Dr. Gaeta talks about, and I never knew it until I came to the seminars, but I wasn't eating properly. I wasn't chewing properly and today I can go to a restaurant, I can eat what I want, I don't have to be embarrassed and I don't have to run to a restroom to rinse my mouth out.*

I also bit him. I always tell this because I did. He said the best thing that happens is when you go to sleep, he hears you snoring. Well, I was snoring so loud one time I guess that I bit him. When I woke up I heard Dr. Gaeta saying "Loretta, let go of my finger. Loretta, would you open your mouth, let go?" I did. I bit him and he still treats me well so that's a plus. That's a good dentist. Thank you.

Now tell me, what kind of looks do you think are on the faces of the people sitting in my audience after they hear those stories? Jaw dropping. That is right. The best part is it did not come from me, the doctor; it came from people just like them!

My dental implant seminars have morphed into a warm, nurturing environment to share and learn. The outcome? Opportunity to serve, educate, create huge revenue, and become the go-to implant dentist in my area.

It still amazes me how many implant dentists are struggling. Traditional advertisers constantly knock at your door making promises of #1 spots on Google and Facebook ads. These are all great, but what about the message? What does it matter if the people who are looking at the ads do not know they need the dental implants?

I had a lady come in to my office recently. After I sat her in the chair, she told me that when she goes out to eat with her friends she just looks at the menu and points out all the things she cannot have. How much would she be willing to pay to eat again if she only knew it was possible?

Becoming a public awareness expert is one of the best investments you can make in yourself, your practice, and your quality of life (fewer patients, more revenue). Taking the time to learn and implement the Public Awareness Seminar system can bring you an abundance of new opportunities to serve, educate, create huge smiles, and bring your patients a greater quality of life.

*"Every time you have to speak,
you are
auditioning for leadership."
- James C. Humes*

CHAPTER 5

CREATING A FLOOD OF NEW IMPLANT PATIENTS

How Can I Attract New Implant Patients?

The Public Awareness Seminar is one of the fundamental tools I teach for community education, but it is not all of them. Remember, people do not know they need dental implants unless they are educated on the consequences of tooth loss. How do you do that? Well, let's see, you will want to create multiple systems of patient education. This is not sales. This is purely educating the patient on the consequences of tooth loss.

In my recent book, *Your Missing Teeth Are Killing You*, I talk about the four main consequences of tooth loss including: bone loss, premature aging, bite force, and shortened life span. The book itself was designed as a patient educational tool. Using this fundamental pillar of educating the potential implant patient is simple and easy for you and your staff to learn.

The first consequence of tooth loss is bone loss. Implants maintain bone size and bone height. If a tooth is lost, without implants the bone in that area will shrink.

Without teeth, when the bone in the jaw begins to shrink it is called "bone resorption," and it can be very dramatic. Wearing dentures can maintain facial form, but the dentures do not arrest the bone shrinkage. Nothing arrests the bone shrinkage, so it constantly gets worse—unless implants are placed.

Once implants are placed, bone loss stops because the implant stimulates the bone. The body thinks it is a tooth. If a person has a cast on an arm or a leg, when the cast is removed after six to eight weeks, the arm or leg looks smaller—muscles actually got smaller because of lack of use, and also the bone shrinks.

The amount of bone loss in the first year after tooth removal is ten times greater than the following years. Also after the first year, bone is lost more quickly from the lower arch than the upper arch.

Here is some education you can do at the chair. I tell this to at least one of my patients almost everyday!

Over time, because of bone loss, dentures do not fit as well as when you first got them. Once your teeth are gone, at first your jawbone has a lot of surface area for the dentures to sit on. Over time, though, your jawbone resorbs and becomes thinner; your dentures no longer fit, and the condition only gets worse. After 25 years you can loose most of the bone that used to hold your teeth in place. Sometimes the mandibular nerve ends up on top of the mandible so that when you bite down it hurts Dental implants avoid this problem altogether by preventing bone loss.

The second consequence of tooth loss is premature aging. Without teeth, the jaw gradually thins and over time the chin may get closer to the nose. (Teeth support the lower one-third of the face.) An interesting long-term study by the National Institute of Health (NIH) concluded that patients who maintain most or all of their natural teeth or have missing teeth replaced by fixed bridge work or have teeth supported by dental implants live 9.8 years longer than those patients who have lost their teeth and wear the usual partials. In addition to improving quality of life, dental implants add years for your patient to live that quality.

We talk about the golden years. Suppose a

couple retire and move to Florida. And do what? Well, they go out to dinner, like Loretta talked about in her testimonial: "I go to the restaurant and I open the menu, I'm looking at the menu and I'm saying to myself, I can't eat this. I can't chew this. I can't chew this." Then she orders pasta or something thing that did not require a lot of chewing. That is why I have these seminars—because I like people to have the quality of life they deserve.

A lot of seniors just get by: "I can chew okay." How good can they really chew? We are supposed to eat fruits and greens, but they cannot.

Here is another way I explain the consequences of tooth loss to my patients:

When you lose you teeth, you lose bone. Bone needs stimulation to maintain form, density, and strength. Tooth loss causes movement of adjacent or opposing teeth. If you lose a couple of teeth, the other teeth migrate into that space so the space. The lower jaw protrudes out farther than the upper jaw so as the chin gets closer to the nose, the lower jaw goes out. Your lips thin, especially the upper lip. Facial muscles sag, contributing to the jowls or creating a "witch's chin": it looks like it sticks out and decreases the overall height of the face.

It is not a pretty picture.

The third consequence of tooth loss is diminished bite force. Bite force deteriorates steadily when wearing dentures. This is significant. An average bite force with molars and natural teeth is 150 to 250 psi (pounds per square inch). The maximum bite force for a denture wearer is less than 50 psi. So as soon as a someone has his teeth out, his bite force goes to 25% of what it was with natural teeth. If a person has only one or two teeth left, these can at least stabilize a denture—but likely as not those teeth are going to come out soon enough. When a person's teeth are all gone and their dentures start flopping around, all they can say is, "Now what?" Remember, even with dentures, patients who have had them for more than 15 years often have a maximum bite force of only 5.6 psi.

Another example. I told a senior woman with dentures to bite down has hard as she could on some carbon articulate paper. She bit down so hard her head was almost shaking, but I easily pulled out the paper. She had no bite force, which means she could not effectively chew. Health consequences of such a reduction in chewing performance are significant, especially because it typically reduces a person's consumption of fruits and vegetables because they are so hard to eat. We simply have to be able to chew our food. It is important.

Additionally, when a person cannot chew or masticate effectively, indigestion can become a problem. If antacids become a solution to indigestion, then soon enough they can be their own problem. Factor in resulting poor nutrition and actual life-expectancy decreases.

However, once someone has dental implants, his or her bite force can increase up to 85%, sometimes up to 300%. People regain significant bite force and dramatically improve the chewing function, bite force retention, and stability.

I have had gastroenterologists tell me that so and so patient needed to be able to chew better, that the patient's inability to masticate her food was making her malnourished.

Although not related to bite force, patients with dental implants regularly report increased taste sensitivity. Dentures often cover and obstruct the palate, covering an area that plays a major role in the sensation of taste. With implants we eliminate the palette plate and snap the denture in, which gives back patients some of their olfactory or taste senses. It is a big quality-of-life issue. Does it affect life expectancy? Absolutely!

Some people cannot wear both dentures all the time. Some people can only wear the top. Most denture wearers have problems with their bottom dentures. And there seems to always be a sore somewhere causing some kind of discomfort and sometimes resulting in difficulty speaking.

In summary, given all the options available in modern dentistry, and given the shortcomings inherent in denture use, dentures are rarely the best solution to tooth loss.

The fourth consequence of tooth loss is a shortened life span. Yes, I admit it sounds dramatic. Unfortunately it is also true—at least if you believe the *National Institute of Health*. After a long-term study they concluded that patients who maintain most or all of their natural teeth, or have missing teeth replaced by fixed bridgework, or have teeth supported by dental implants, live longer than patients who wear removable dentures or partials. How much longer? How about 9.8 years longer. In other words, wearing only dentures can actually take about 10 years off your life.

How can this happen? How can a simple appliance that has been around forever and is supposed to *help* you put you in danger? The answer is simple: it is all about eating. Seniors, who need good nutrition to remain strong and healthy, do not get the calories or the nutrients they need when they wear dentures. This lack of proper nutrition robs them of almost 10 years of their lives. Luckily, there is something you can do to get back those years: you can replace your dentures with dental implants.

In 1984, four dental scientists in Denmark set out to determine the processes involved in the "early signs of accelerated aging." They thought that by determining the early signs and addressing them they could prevent some disabilities. They decided to look closely at tooth loss. From 1984 to 2006 they studied and tracked the health of 573 people who were in then in their 70s. These scientists even took into account different factors like income, health conditions like high blood pressure, and how tired or physically active each person was.

They found that by age 75 a person who had lost all of his or her teeth was almost three times more likely to be physically disabled than a person with twenty or more teeth. Even more startling was that someone with no teeth had a 265% higher risk of dying sooner than a person who still had teeth. The study showed that the average person who had no natural teeth lived for about 11.5 more years after the study began. Meanwhile, the average person who had 20 or more teeth lived for about 17.5 more years.

Researchers from Italy did a study of 1,124 people in their early 70s who were all city-dwellers and healthy enough to live at home. These researchers wanted to see if there were differences among three groups: those who had enough natural teeth (at least 16), those who did not have enough natural teeth (had fewer than 16), and those who wore some kind of dentures (whether removable or fixed, partial or complete).

The results were rather interesting. First, both the seniors with an adequate number of natural teeth and the seniors who wore dentures were able to complete their day-to-day activities. But people with enough natural teeth were more likely to say that they had satisfying social relationships than either people with dentures or the people who had few teeth. Also, people with enough teeth were less likely to need health services than either the people who wore dentures or the people who did not have enough teeth.

Ten years after the first study, the researchers checked government records to see what had happened to the people in the study. They found out that over half of the people who had participated were still alive. However, there were differences in the numbers of people who had survived in each group. Of the seniors who had enough natural teeth, 67% were still alive. Of the seniors who had dentures, 55% of them were still alive. For the people who did not have enough teeth and who were not using any type of dentures, 52% of them were still alive.

At Leisure World retirement community in California, 5,611 older adults were studied for an average of 9 years. These were well-educated, upper-middle class people with an average age of 81. This study started in 1992 and the researchers took into account all the things you might think would affect longevity, including activity, whether the seniors had other ailments, and whether they smoked or drank. Some of the seniors were very healthy— one person even lived to be 108!

This study showed that teeth mattered a lot for longevity. In this study, the researchers looked specifically at a person's risk of dying. Unfortunately, individuals with no teeth (even those who wore dentures) had a 30% higher risk of death compared to the seniors who had 20 or more natural teeth. Almost all (90% percent) of the seniors who had fewer than 16 teeth had dentures they could wear. Whether they live in Italy or in the U.S., seniors with teeth tend to live longer.

In my system for education I teach you to stick to these four consequences when educating your patients about tooth loss. There are many more consequences that could be included, but these are the main ones. When it comes to educating the public, consistency is a critical factor as well. You want the education they receive outside your office to be consistent with the continued education they received from your staff when they come into your office. If you are teaching your community about consequences your staff is not yet familiar with, you risk losing credibility. Having your staff learn these four consequences of tooth loss is not a difficult task and can create an extension of the education your patients receive before they even call the office.

An important part of educating your community starts within your current practice. I bet it is safe to say there are many patients in your practice who would be a perfect candidates for dental implants. I stress to my staff that everyone with tooth loss needs to know the consequences. We talk about tooth loss, bone loss, bite force, and premature aging everyday!

"The most important thing in communication is to hear what isn't being said."
- Peter F. Drucker

How Can I Reach the People Who have Lost Teeth?

All you need to locate as many new implant patients you want is to learn public awareness. Public awareness is all about education, not selling.

I know you may not know how to do this, and that is Ok because I am going to show you how you can. As a matter of fact, I'll even bet that by following my simple and easy system you can generate an additional $250,000 in new implant cases over the next 12 months.

You may be thinking that there is no way simple public awareness can get those results, but I can assure you I have a system in place which generates at least $75,000-$100,000 of new implant cases *every time* I use it.

You may not think you have any time in your practice for new systems. How can you possibly even think of adding on another component to the practice when you are already seeing 20 or more patients a day? Maybe so, but what kind of patients are these? Mostly general dentistry? Wouldn't you rather be placing and restoring implant cases under IV sedation? This type of atmosphere is total serenity! A dentist's favorite sound is a patient snoring! When they are relaxed, so are you. You can do a better job. Some patients will think you are a hero because with IV sedation they have the most satisfying and relaxing dental experience they have ever had! They become raving fans and a huge referral source.

I want you to imagine what it would feel like to have three implant cases in the morning, finish at noon, and be out on the golf course (or wherever you want to be that afternoon) by 1:00 p.m. That is very possible and I am going to show you how.

How Can You Generate Implant Patients through Public Awareness Seminars?

The first place to start is to realize that times are changing. The way people make buying decisions is completely different than it was five years ago. We are moving towards a time when the way we present our services and sell our products needs to be presented as a *need* instead of a *want*.

I do not have to elaborate on the financial

effects of our recent economy because you have probably already experienced this first hand in your practice. On the flip side, we are just entering a time where we are actually going to experience an abundance of opportunity. AARP recently reported, "We are entering an epidemic of tooth loss in the coming years." Our population is growing older and tooth loss is directly related to age. Regardless of what condition the economy is in, people are going to be losing their teeth in the coming years and they are going to need to do something about it.

There is an abundance of opportunity all around. Recognizing where the opportunity lies and positioning yourself to take advantage of it is the key.

"If you just communicate, you can get by.
But if you communicate skillfully,
you can work miracles"
- Jim Rohn

As I said in the earlier sections of this book, baby boomers and seniors make up a fast-growing segment of the population, and will need dental implants. It is also important to recognize that baby boomers and seniors are part of a different generation, and learning how to properly communicate with them is vital.

Baby boomers and seniors have seen it all. They have lived through the Great Depression, world wars, scandals, and many recessions. They are not generally going to make decisions on the spot, and will frequently "sleep on it." They need to see true value and need. They consider shopping a social event and prefer to do so in the morning hours. They are savers and investors. They seek personal attention, and buy products and services based on quality and brand name.

A couple generations ago, dentures were pretty much expected as you got older. In fact, in the 1800s, because dentures were the only option at the time for tooth loss, it was common for a couple to receive a pair of dentures as a wedding gift!

Today, Implant Dentistry has changed everything and has now become the standard of care for tooth loss. The problem is that many of the seniors and baby boomers have not been educated on the benefits of dental implants—or even what dental implants are!

In fact, many of them have no idea that if they leave a few missing teeth in the back of their mouth, serious consequences can occur. Public awareness has not caught up with the speed of innovations in Implant Dentistry. Educating them (and your community) about the four major consequences of tooth loss will be not only an eye-opening reality, but an enormous opportunity for you. Once they realize how tooth loss can affect their health and quality of life they will be motivated to make a change. After they recognize the problem, seeing dental implants as the solution and new standard of care will be obvious. Price will not be the focus; solving their problem will.

Learning how to generate public awareness though implant seminars can be one of the most valuable things you implement in your practice for the coming years. Public Awareness Seminars provide one of the best ways to reach your community for four reasons:

-Your community gets a chance to know and like you.

-They get educated about problems they never knew were related to tooth loss. You are not selling to them.

-You create social proof. Other people look at what others are doing. Seminars are a great way for people to learn first hand from others in the room about their experience.

-You establish a sense of community by creating a comfortable, non-pressure almost social setting. We're all in this together.

All these ways of communicating especially appeal to baby boomers and seniors because of the way they prefer to make decisions in the buying process.

"Hi I'm Dr. Christopher Donato, and I'm in Tampa, Florida just outside my office. I just got back from doing a public awareness seminar with Dr. Gaeta. A few months back we started off talking about putting on an implant seminar. So Dr. Gaeta and his staff helped me put together a structure and planned out what we were going to do for the seminar and everything leading up to it. So Dr. Gaeta actually did the seminar with me where we were both speaking. I was the main speaker and he was there talking as a colleague. It was really nice because we were there talking and kicking it back and forth with one another. It really added a lot of value for the people who attended. We did a really good job and got a lot of new implant patients from it."

Why Should You Learn How to Do Implant Seminars?

1 - You have an opportunity to establish your credibility.

2 - You build rapport because potential patients personally meet you, and possibly some of your staff as well. A hand shake goes a long way.

3 - You can educate many people at once, reaching far more at the same time than you can reach one-on-one.

4 - Provide focused attention. You are taking people out of their busy lives and putting them in a non-distracted learning environment.

5 -You can answer questions on the spot.

6 -You can personally invite potential patients to the office for a consult, or even close implant cases at the event.

Learning the ins and outs of how to conduct your own Public Awareness Seminar can make a significant impact in new implant cases. The financial rewards come at about a 10-to-1 return on investment.

"Take advantage of every opportunity to practice your communication skills so that when important occasions arise, you will have the gift, the style, the sharpness, the clarity, and the emotions to affect other people"
– Jim Rohn

For example, every time I put on a Public Awareness Seminar I generate approximately $100,000 in new dental implant cases. Every time. This means I always get back at least a 700-800% return on my investment.

I want to share with you a story about Roxanne, a 38-year-old female patient I treated recently.

Roxanne came into my office because she already, at 38, had an upper denture and it was bothering her. I was distraught after examining her. If you think about it, what, normally, would be the probability of her living into her 90s? It is 86%. So she is going to have to live another 50 or so years with an upper denture, constantly loosing bone, with minimal bite force and not being able to eat anything she wants.

The most disturbing part of her situation was that the dentist who took out her teeth *never* explained to her the consequences of tooth loss *before* he took her teeth out! He *never* told her she would continue to lose bone for the rest of her life, which could lead to premature aging, inability to chew, and ultimately (according to a Harvard study) take up to ten years off her life!

As I explained all of this to Roxanne, she naturally is did not taking it very well—especially since her teeth were removed four years ago. I could clearly see she had already lost significant bone in her upper jaw, which was the reason for her loose dentures. On top of that, her face had already started to prematurely age due to that bone loss.

I tell this story about Roxanne because this could easily describe one of your patients. We all have seen them. Her condition could have been completely prevented if she had been educated through public awareness about the consequences of tooth loss! If she had learned ahead of time about all the serious consequences of tooth loss then it would have been very easy for me to present her with the solution.

I am certain that if, prior to having her teeth removed, Roxanne had attended one of my Public Awareness Seminars, where she would have learned that a person can appear years older in only months following so much as having a single tooth pulled, and that dental implants are the only choice to replace the root and prevent the consequences, she would have at least made a more educated choice. Moreover, I am also certain that price would not have been the focus of her concern—solving her problem would have been!

In this situation both Roxanne and the dentist lost out. Roxanne was not properly educated by her dentist; therefore she did not receive the best possible treatment for her problem and now has to suffer unfortunate health consequences. The dentist, on the other hand, missed out on a significant opportunity as a result of not educating his patient. If he had explained to her the consequences of tooth loss and that dental implants are the primary treatment of choice, he would have created a treatment plan that would have resulted in over 12 times the revenue while at the same time creating the quality of life Roxanne deserved.

There are so many people suffering right now in our communities who have no idea how much of their present problems directly result from tooth loss and bone loss. Take Roxanne for instance. She had no idea that tooth loss, if left untreated, caused bone loss for the rest of her life. She had no idea that she would experience premature aging (the wrinkled face syndrome) for the same reason. At only 38 years old, do you think she would have been concerned? **Yes!**

This is why I love teaching the skill of creating Public Awareness Seminars. It is very rewarding for me to be directly involved in changing the quality of life for others. It has also created very lucrative opportunities.

CHAPTER 6

CREATING EFFECTIVE PUBLIC AWARENESS SEMINARS

How Do You Put On a Public Awareness Seminar?

Putting on your own Public Awareness Seminar can be fun, rewarding, and incredibly lucrative. The best part is that you can train your staff to do everything for you!

There are three main sections to a Public Awareness Seminar: Pre-Seminar Planning, Day of Seminar Activities, and Post-Seminar Follow-up.

The Pre-Seminar planning includes a number of things you will need to organize, including the following:

> Selecting a strategic date and time.
>
> Finding the perfect location and negotiating terms.
>
> Planning a specific room setup.
>
> Executing the marketing campaign.
>
> Choosing your team and delegating tasks.
>
> Managing the registration process.

Ordering attendee materials and gifts.

Creating the PowerPoint presentation.

Contacting patients with testimonials to attend the event.

Strategizing IT and multi-media set-up.

Organizing dental implant models.

Going over final arrangements and room check.

In my step-by-step 6 Figure Seminar System I show you exactly what you do in each phase of the above list so you can literally hand it to your office manager or other competent staff member to organize the entire event while you continue seeing existing patients, never missing a beat.
You can get more information at:
www.publicawarenessacademy.com

The next phase of the seminar is the Day of Seminar Activities These include:

Final setup and room check.

Making sure staff is clear about their

duties.

Conduct a morning huddle.

Final speaking preparation.

Delivering a successful presentation.

Scheduling consults.

Wrap up/close down.

The debrief lunch.

Finally, the last phase of the seminar is Post Seminar Follow-Up which includes:

Converting attendee implant consults into patients.

Treatment planning strategies.

Continued patient educational materials.

Follow-up marketing letters.

Patient and financial tracking reports.

My goal is to make this so easy that you can have your staff do everything for you! Remember, your main focus is to educate your community. This Public Awareness Seminar system will not only provide a vehicle for you to do that but also be a means for generating new implant patients.

You do not need to get bogged down in trying to create from scratch your own Pubic Awareness Seminar event. Learn my system, then delegate as much of the work as you can.

What If I Have No Idea How to Speak to an Audience?

For many people, the thought of speaking in front of other people is not pleasant. It wasn't for me! And, just like when I got started, some of you may not have that much experience speaking (or maybe none at all), and that is Ok.

I want to share with you some strategies that help me when I get in front of an audience at my seminars. Remember, I had absolutely no prior speaking experience. Since beginning, I have changed my mindset about speaking. I now look at myself as an expert in the field and only here to teach and to educate others.

Here are 5 Things I do before speaking to an audience:

1 - I say this mantra to myself over and over: "I am a teacher, here to serve and educate others." (I repeat this to myself about 20 times before I go on stage.)

2 - I go for a morning run. I love to do this because it not only helps reduce any anxiety I may be experiencing but it gives me an oxygen boost so I can think clearly. It helps put me in a great state!

3 - I wear my favorite speaking suit. This may sound ridiculous to you, but I actually have a suit coat that I wear every time I put on my seminars. Call it my "lucky suit coat," or just one that makes me feel comfortable every time I wear it. Not only will I know I won't have to deal with any wardrobe issues, but when I wear it I've impressed in my mind that now I am in a speaking mode.

4 - I have a good breakfast. This is very important every day of your life, but especially when you are going to need some extra sustained physical and mental energy on a particular day. I make sure that I eat a good breakfast that includes lots of greens. I take a powdered green drink every day that is loaded with energy-packed greens. I also have a vegetarian protein drink as well. My favorite is

the Vega brand. If I still feel the need for an extra boost before going on stage, I drink a Zip Fizz, which is loaded with B vitamins. Remember, you need to keep your energy up on stage. You are not just a speaker, you are something of an entertainer. Do you remember the high school teacher who bored you to sleep? You do not want to be like him (or her) when speaking to your audience.

5 - I connect with two or three audience members before going on stage. I will walk in the room to have a staff huddle about 30 minutes before speaking. At this time I may introduce myself to some of the early-bird arrivals. When it is time for me to start my presentation, I feel more comfortable, like I already know a few people who are there. Sometimes when I have to call on the audience for some reason or other, I might ask one of them if he or she would like to say anything. It reinforces our earlier introduction. It also makes me feel more comfortable. I also know it helps the audience see that I can connect with them.

I always make the seminars fun, casual, and educational. I tell everyone if they have a question to not hesitate, just raise their hand and I will be happy to answer. I always repeat any question so that other attendees can hear it, as well as my answer. I like to walk around a little bit and keep it casual. A big smile reinvigorates everyone and lets them know that I am there to help educate them.

"You can speak well if your tongue can deliver the message of your heart."
- John Ford

Do I Need a Large Staff to Put On a Seminar?

Some of you may have a small staff, and some of you may have more staff available. It is important that you chose the right individuals for each role at your Public Awareness Seminar. I have a process for this, and have had incredible results.

First, let us start by listing the different roles you will need to fill for your seminar. I have broken my seminar personnel needs into seven roles: IT/AV person, Registration/Check-in person, Greeter, Runners, Introducer, Appointment Setter, and Team Leader.

You do not have to worry about having a separate person for each role; one person can always fulfill two (or more).

Let us start with the IT/AV person. This may be an outside contractor or a staff member who has good technology skills. He or she will be responsible for setting up and operating all of the AV equipment during the seminar. This includes the projector, laptop computer, remote control for the PowerPoint presentation, and the microphone system. It is best to choose a highly detailed-oriented staff member. My main assistant, Dawn, is generally the one who handles this role for me. She is good with tools and equipment, is techy, and is very smart and can usually figure out any issues on her own.

Next, you will need one or two people for the Registration/Check-in team. They will be responsible for checking-in your attendees, giving them a nametag and their welcome packet and information. The also reminding attendees about the free consultation, then direct them into the room. Generally this team is an attendee's first point of contact. I usually choose for this role staff who already work directly with patients, who have a bubbly personality and big smile.

Next is your Greeter. This person stands by the entrance to the seminar room and helps direct and seat your guests. You will want this person to roll out the red carpet for your attendees. The Greeter should be someone who likes to please, serve, and accommodate. Again you will want to choose someone who is used to working directly with patients and making them feel comfortable.

Your Runners. I choose staff for this role who are quick thinkers and quick on their toes.

Runners are the ones who constantly scan the room for raised hands and who can get right in there with the microphone. They also show the implant models and know all the ins and outs about them. While one Runner is responsible for the audience microphone, the other is responsible for passing the dental implant models around and answering any questions the attendees may have about them. If you do not have enough staff for two Runners, then one person usually works fine.

Next is your Introducer. This is an important role because this person will actually start the seminar by welcoming everyone and introducing you, the Doctor. They will read a prepared script and stand in front of the audience with the microphone. You will want this to be your top personality in the office— confident, well spoken, and poised. Generally, I will have this person dress a step up from the normal dress code because they are getting up in front of the audience. They need to feel comfortable speaking in front of an audience and be able to follow the prepared script.

Your Appointment Setters. These staff sit in the back of the room with the lap top computers, which are hooked up directly to our scheduling system. They set appointments for the free consults after the seminar. I usually have the same staff who do the scheduling in the office, do this here. Keep in mind, you can have the same person who was a greeter at the door be an appointment setter. You do not need separate people for all these positions.

Finally, your Team Leader. This person needs to make sure everything runs smoothly and is familiar with everything that should be going on, and when. You want to be confident that the person in this role can run things without you. This could be your office manager, or someone else who is good at multi-tasking. Possibly this person has been more involved with the overall event management and is familiar with all its ins and outs. Your Team Leader will make sure everything is taken care of: the food, the room layout, the staff members, the attendee materials, and anything else that needs attention.

Those are all the main staff roles that make the seminar happen. Remember, you can have each staff member be responsible for multiple roles. You can also hire outside contractors to help, say for IT/AV. I do this frequently with my IT guy, Marc, if my assistant, Dawn, is not available. Marc handles all of my office networking, so when I have a public seminar I hire him for a few hours to run all the equipment.

Selecting the right staff for the right role in your seminars is important. So finding dependable, organized, and pleasant staff is the key. You want your staff to do everything for you, so if you take some time in the beginning to get a good regular team in place, your seminars will flow easily!

What Do I Talk about at My Public Awareness Seminar?

I use a simple PowerPoint presentation to educate my audience about the four consequences of tooth loss, which I have talked about throughout this book.

I usually start by introducing myself and giving some personal information for credibility. I include family photos as well as logos from associations and my achievements in dentistry.

I then present the problem of tooth loss by using third-party statistics. This way I show

how the average age is rising, tooth loss is growing, and more and more people will be losing teeth in the coming years. By using third-party statistics I position myself as the messenger, not as only presenting my personal opinion. It also helps educate the audience about the big picture and their generation as a whole rather than seem to point a finger at them personally. This maintains the feeling of a safe and nurturing environment.

Then I talk about each of the consequences of tooth loss. I include graphics and photos of each pillar of tooth loss so the audience can visually get an idea of what is happening when a tooth is lost. At this time in the PowerPoint presentation I have one of my staff members go around the room with dental implant models. During this part of the presentation I will also have my special guests present their dental implant stories. These stories provide the social proof about the importance of what I have been talking about. Testimonials are priceless. They alone have engaged some of my audience so much that sometimes people get up in the middle of my presentation and go to the back of the room to immediately schedule a dental implant consultation!

Finally, I conclude my PowerPoint presentation

by including a Q & A section. I take the top ten questions I get asked about dental implants and answer them for the audience. Some of these include: Am I a candidate for dental implants? How much do dental implants cost? Do dental implants hurt? Are dental implants covered under insurance? Sometimes, I'll even ask my testimonials to get up again and answer some of these questions—especially when talking about personal concerns such as pain. Many people respond better to someone who actually went through the process than the doctor just giving his facts.

How Long Should a Public Awareness Seminar Last?

Generally my seminars last around an hour and a half from start to finish. It depends on how long I have the room rental and how engaged my audience is in asking questions. You want to make sure that I give myself enough time to deliver my information, but short enough that people do not get bored or lose interest from sitting too long. I try to be fun and entertaining during all of my seminars for this exact reason. I have found that the more I am "myself", the more people respond to me and enjoy the seminar.

What Do I Do When the Public Awareness Seminar is Over?

Following the Public Awareness Seminars, as a thank-you gift, I offer free dental implant consultations to all attendees. I have staff with lap tops in the back of the room schedule appointments right then and there for that afternoon, which I keep open for consults. After all the attendees leave and everyone helps clean up, I take the staff who attended and the people who gave testimonials out for a debriefing lunch. At the lunch I ask everyone to give me their feedback on how they thought the seminar went—good and bad. I also ask them to talk about anything that happened they would like to share

Remember, there is an abundance of people in your community right now who are suffering from the consequences of tooth loss. They have money to spend, but don't yet realize their problems are tooth related. Through Public Awareness Seminars, in a friendly environment where they feel they are being taught not sold, you can educate your community about what is really happening to them.

I have seen how Public Awareness Seminars convert new implant patients at a dramatic rate. People who are educated about their problems make decisions to solve their problems. I have seen the shock on so many people's faces when they learn what tooth loss is doing to them. At the end of a seminar, often there is a line down the center of the room of people waiting to make an appointment at my office.

The greatest part of the seminars is knowing that you are helping your community in a positive way. Not only are you going to be rewarded financially but there are people who, if not for your seminars, would continue to suffer unnecessary physical, health, and financial burdens.

"Criticism is something we can avoid easily by saying nothing, doing nothing, and being nothing."
– Aristotle

CHAPTER 7

DON'T WAIT UNTIL YOUR TICKET GETS PUNCHED

Why Do You Need to Know Your "Why"?

I've been practicing dentistry for 27 years. Every morning I wake up and take ten minutes to reflect on my "why": Why do I practice dentistry? Why do I commit my life to service?

I grew up in the restaurant business working for my father, Joe Senior. I worked there, along with my mom, Josephine, my entire childhood and up until I graduated from dental school (and even beyond that). Growing up in the restaurant business made me realize that I am on this earth to serve and help others. Life is service.

That is my true "why": helping others, treating everyone I encounter as if they were a member of my family.

What are your life goals?

My goal is to leave a legacy vision that last well beyond my lifetime. As Tony Robbins says, "It is not what you get in this life, it is who you become." You are not going to be remembered for the big house, the fancy car, the boat, and all the material things; you are going to be remembered for the lives you have impacted. I have discovered that Implant Dentistry impacts lives. It is a life-changing profession for the practitioner; it is a life-changing experience for your patients.

Let me tell you about Josie, a 93-year-old female patient of mine. She came into the office using a walker. She had a nasal cannula and wheeled around a portable oxygen tank. Reviewing her medical history I saw she has COPD and A-Fib. After finishing her implant treatment and getting her implant-supported lower denture, she came in for her first week post-op. She looked at me with a big smile on her face and said, "Finally I can eat what I want to!" I have to tell you, there is nothing better than seeing the satisfaction of a senior, who has all these ailments, who can finally chew again! This is the true "mission" of an implant dentist.

Why is It Important to Be in the Service of Others?

I would like to tell you another story. It is about a patient named Sirl. Yes, that is his name, and he is 96 years old. I just finished his case a couple weeks ago. It was only two implants—lower anterior with locators. At his final insertion appointment for his lower implant-supported denture I videotaped him trying to get the denture out. He actually moaned and groaned trying to get it out with his finger until he finally figured out how. When he came back a week later for a check-up he looked at me with a tear in his eye. He grabbed my hand with both of his and expressed with such gratitude, "Thank you, Dr. Gaeta. I can eat again."

No amount of money gives me that deep feeling of fulfillment as when I see patients like Sirl with a big smile on his face, literally looking like a changed man, a new person. In those magic moments I think there's nothing better.

"The most important single ingredient in the formula of success is knowing how to get along with people."
- Theodore Roosevelt

What if I Don't Have Time to Implement New Systems in My Practice?

It was December 9, 2013, a Sunday afternoon. I live in Sarasota, Florida and the Tampa Bay Buccaneers were playing at home that day at 1:30 p.m. I called my youngest son, Joey, to see if he wanted to go to the game with me. He said he had too much homework and could not go. So I decided to ride my motorcycle to the game. They played Philly that day and it was a great game. On my way home I was run off the road on the interstate by semi tractor-trailer that I believe did not even see me. I was flown to Blake Hospital Trauma Hospital in Bradenton Florida and was in a coma for two weeks. On four occasions I was given my Last Rites. The doctors removed my spleen and I ended up with nine broken ribs, a shattered clavicle, and a fractured scapula.

I had almost died. What if God had taken me then? The message I am so passionate about would never have been perpetuated.

With all the love and prayer from family, friends, and my church, God decided to keep me on this earth. I believe one of His main reasons was so that I could help get this message out to the world! After the accident, when I met Sr. Judy from St. Thomas More Church in Sarasota, she said to me "You ain't done yet, boy!"

The accident reminded me that the clock is always ticking.

What about you? Whatever your goals in life, shouldn't you pursue them now, with great passion, and not wait until later, when "the time is right"? The time may never be right, and there may come a moment when the door of opportunity closes forever.

Why tell yourself that you do not have time to do something that will better your life or get you closer to your goals? As a result of my accident I realized that all of the knowledge inside me could have been lost forever that day. The worst would have been that I had not already created my legacy and that I would have left many goals unattained.

Learning how to master time management can significantly increase the productive time in your day. I focus a great deal on this and can say that it directly contributes to my success as a dentist. We are continually confronted with so many distractions that suck up our time like a vampire—everything from staff interruptions, cell phone calls, social media, and email. It is very important to become disciplined and somewhat guarded with your time. Realize your hourly value and choose to do only the things that move you forward towards a goal. You will be surprised at how much time you can gain in a day if you take a minute to analyze where all your time is used everyday, then organize your priorities.

By taking action you will be surprised at how much more you can accomplish. Therefore, learning new systems and training staff will be completely possible—as well as increasing your revenue.

Why Should the Joy Be in The Journey?

I have good and bad days—as we all do. That's life! But if I keep my "why" of service to others, especially the seniors, as my premise for practicing, I feel the joy of having given them that little bit better quality of life as they enter their twilight years.

I've been a big fan of the motivational speaker Tony Robbins for years. There are two primary needs he states that keep us going: you have to *grow* <u>and</u> you have to *give*.

Grow: constantly improve and get better and better at what you do.

Give: give to others, live a life of service to mankind.

Tony Robbins often says that the only time you fail is when you quit. You may achieve an "unexpected outcome" (that is, not be as successful as you had planned), then what do you do? You change your approach and try again. If you still do not get the outcome you desire, what do you do? You change your approach again—and try again, . . . and again . . . and again. In essence, you do not *ever* give up. You persist until you achieve your desired outcome. Tony Robbins has a saying that I have adopted in my life when faced with challenges: THIS SHALL MAKE ME MORE!!!! So if you ever become challenged just remember this saying... It always helps in creating *purpose* for the challenge you are faced with.

"Over time, our choices become habits of the heart.
And, more than any other factor, these habits of the heart affect our time and the quality of our lives."
- Steven Covey

What is the First Thing You Need to Do?

Chances are you have arrived at this point in the book because you are serious about getting new implant patients and doing what you really love to do! Congratulations! You now have information most others do not—and this can help establish you as the perceived expert in your community.

You will want to choose your seminar team right away. I bet there is a key person in your office to whom you can delegate the seminar coordination. Start thinking about which of your staff members would be good for which roles.

Another great idea is to take a look at your current database. See if you can sort out all the patients who wear dentures. This can be your initial group to invite to your first seminar. Contact assisted living facilities, mobile home parks, senior centers, nursing services, and so forth.

I get my best response from newspaper advertising. I scheduled a series of display ads running two weeks prior to my first seminar. In my product, 6 Figure Implant Seminar Secrets,

I give you step-by-step information to help you put on your first seminar. I include handouts and checklists for your staff so they know exactly what to do.

Remember, you're first seminar does not have to be perfect. People will show up no matter what. As long as your message is in the right place and you create value for them, you will most likely close some deals.

Getting started sometimes is the hardest part, and the most important part. You do not have to worry about every detail. Just create your first event and serve the people who come with the knowledge you know can save years of their lives. You will have fun, the attendees will be grateful for the information you provide, and you will learn as you go along.

If you are interested in skipping ahead and getting your hands on my done-for-you seminar system you can visit:
www.publicawarenessacademy.com
where you learn more about my comprehensive step-by-step, hold-you-by-the-hand money-generating implant seminar system.

Why Do You Want to Be a Multiple 7-Figure Dentist?

How do you define success? Is it money? Fancy cars? A big house? A swimming pool in your backyard? A multiple seven-figure annual income? What is true fulfillment? The dictionary defines fulfillment as satisfaction or happiness as a result of fully valuing one's abilities or character. Can you have success without true fulfillment? John Belushi was successful but was he fulfilled? No. He overdosed on drugs and killed himself!

The bigger a practice you have does not just mean more money to buy a luxury car and a large house. It means you are changing the lives of more and more people, making a difference on this earth, saving lives that would otherwise be full of suffering and hardship, allowing a grandmother or grandfather to watch their kids grow up and not be a victim of a shortened life span because of their inability to chew and eat properly. That is what being a three million-dollar dentist is all about.

The money is a by-product of the life-changing experience your patients have with Implant Dentistry. You create *your* personal legacy of service that will last way beyond your lifetime.

Your patients will never forget, and will become raving fans of you and your dental team. Let us together go out and spread this message of how Implant Dentistry can change lives.

Go to
www.publicawarenessacademy.com *to*
learn more about how
you can generate an abundance of new
implant patients today.

"What you become directly influences what you get"
- Jim Rohn

NOW IT IS TIME TO TAKE ACTION!

CHAPTER 8

SPREADING THE MESSAGE WORLDWIDE

Changing lives is the motivation for promoting education about Implant Dentistry and the consequences of tooth loss.

In my quest to perpetuate the message about bone loss and the life-changing effects of Implant Dentistry, I asked myself how do I get this message out worldwide? First, I created my Public Awareness Seminars. The next step is for others, like yourself, to do the same. The more we educate, the more Implant Dentistry inevitably grows, the more we can be of service.

First, you will want to get my system "6-Figure Seminar Secrets," in which I share everything I know and have used to generate a multitude of implant patients—and how, therefore, you can, too. Just go to www.publicawarenessacademy.com.

Next, the world needs your help. Approximately 20% of the world's population is suffering from tooth loss; those numbers are only going to grow. I highly recommend participating in the nonprofit organization WDIAO (World Dental Implant Awareness Organization).

WDIAO is a 501.C3 nonprofit organization dedicated to spreading the message about tooth loss, bone loss, its consequences, and the life-changing benefits of dental implants. Sponsorship proceeds will be used to perpetuate this message worldwide. We want to see billboards in Australia, New Guinea, Italy, France, Germany, Spain, and Russia... Worldwide!!!

WDIAO is currently in need of implant dentists who wish to partner with it. By becoming a part of this special mission there are numerous benefits to your practice. Join us in spreading the message around the world about tooth loss.

Get involved with WDIAO
www.WDIAO.org

ENDNOTES

1. U.S. Department of Health and Human Services, National Institutes of Health, National Institute of Dental and Craniofacial Research. (2004). *Tooth Loss in Seniors (Age 65 and Over)* Retrieved from http://www.nidcr.nih.gov/DataStatistics/Find DataByTopic/ToothLoss/ToothLossSeniors65a ndOlder

2. U.S. Department of Health and Human Services, National Institutes of Health, National Institute of Dental and Craniofacial Research. (2004). *Tooth Loss in Seniors (Age 65 and Over)* Retrieved from http://www.nidcr.nih.gov/DataStatistics/Find DataByTopic/ToothLoss/ToothLossSeniors65a ndOlder

3. *Tooth Loss.* (Introduction) In Oral Health U.S., 2002 , NIDCR/CDC Data Resource Center. Retrieved from http://drc.hhs.gov/report/pdfs/section4-toothloss.pdf

4. *Tooth Loss.* (Section 4.4) In Oral Health U.S., 2002 , NIDCR/CDC Data Resource Center. Retrieved from

http://drc.hhs.gov/report/pdfs/section4-toothloss.pdf

5. *Dental Implants*. American Association of Oral and Maxillofacial Surgeons. Retrieved from http://www.aaoms.org/conditions-and-treatments/dental-implants/

6. Achermann, G. (2012, May) *How will Dentistry look in 2020?* Presented at Capital Markets Day, Amsterdam, The Netherlands. Retrieved http://www.straumann.com/content/dam/internet/straumann_com/Resources/investor-relations/publications-and-reports/capital-markets-day-2012/How%20will%20dentistry%20in%202020%20look_Straumann%20CMD2012_Achermann.pdf

7. Life Expectancy at Birth by Race and Sex 1930-2010. In *infoplease*. Retrieved from http://www.infoplease.com/ipa/A0005148.html

8. Baby Boomers Retire. (2010, December). *Pew Research Center*. Retrieved from http://www.pewresearch.org/daily-number/baby-boomers-retire/

9. Knickman, J,. Hunt, K., Snell, E, et al.

Wealth Patterns Among Elderly Americans: Implications For Health Care Affordability. *Health Affairs*. Retrieved from http://content.healthaffairs.org/content/22/3/168.full

10. A Perfect Body or a Perfect Smile? (2012) American Academy of Cosmetic Dentistry. Retrieved from http://www.aacd.com/index.php?module=cms&page=1260

11. Levin, R, and Judy, K. W. M., Trends in implant dentistry. In *Dental Economics*. Retrieved from http://www.dentaleconomics.com/articles/print/volume-100/issue-12/features/trends-in-implant-dentistry.html

12. *Dental Implants*. American Association of Oral and Maxillofacial Surgeons. Retrieved from http://www.aaoms.org/conditions-and-treatments/dental-implants/

FREE GIFT FOR YOU!
Dr. Gaeta's entire Transcribed Dental Implant Seminar

Host: Good morning, everyone. How's everybody today.

Audience: Okay, I am.

Host: Just one person is good today? We want to thank you all so much for coming this morning. We want to welcome you to seminar. Before we get started, we wanted to briefly introduce you to Dr. Gaeta's team. If you all would like to briefly mention your names.

- Hi, my name is Donna and I'm Dr. Gaeta's dental hygienist
- Good morning, my name is Pamela and I'm Dr. Gaeta's dental assistant
- Good morning, I'm Kolleen, I'm Dr. Gaeta's wife
- Good morning, my name is Tammy

- Hello, my name is Kyle. I'm a dental assistant.
- Hi, my name is Heather, and I'm Dr. Gaeta's assistant

I want to bring to your attention that in your package, you received a confidential attendee survey. At the end of this seminar, if you would be so kind as to fill that out and turn that in to us so we can better serve you in the future.

I want to give you a brief background on your speaker today, Dr. Gaeta. He's originally from Omaha, Nebraska and is a graduate of Creighton University's , School of Dental Science. Dr. Gaeta moved to the Sarasota area in 1988 and has been placing dental implants for over 20 years. In 1999, Dr. Gaeta achieved Board Certification status with the American Board of Oral Implantology and fewer than 500 dentists worldwide that have achieved such status. Dr. Gaeta has a relentless passion to serve. He's an author and with his wife, Kolleen, have four children and three dogs. Dr. Gaeta is also a tri-athlete and marathon runner.

Without further ado, I'd like to introduce you to Dr. Joseph Gaeta.

Dr. Gaeta: Good morning. Thank you, team. How is everybody this morning? It was a beautiful day outside today wasn't it, on the way in? Hopefully, it gets warmer. Again, thank you for coming.

My objective today is to give everyone a better understanding of implant dentistry. Implant dentistry has made an unbelievable shift in the amount of progress in the research and development of implant dentistry. It has evolved and become the gold standard for tooth replacement.

A long time ago when we were

younger, implants didn't work. There was so much suffering over the years where people just can't chew. After having your teeth removed bite force goes to only 25% of what it was with natural teeth, so you become a dental cripple. I trained under Carl Misch, who was the Pope's dentist, the late Pope John Paul.

He would always talk about going to see his 90-year old grandmother in a convalescent home, how she couldn't chew and how people in the convalescent home can't chew when they lose their teeth. In fact, I have a mobile denture care service where I go to convalescent homes. If you have loved ones or friends that are in a convalescent home and they can't come to the dental office, I go there and help them with their denture problems.

Over the years, I said something has to be done, so I've created an organization called the Public Awareness Academy. It's a public awareness association for implant dentistry and my goal with the academy is to empower other implant dentists to create awareness in their communities, to have seminars like this, to teach the public about the magic and the miracle of implant dentistry.

I'm writing a book called Your Missing Teeth Are Killing You. Today, I will answer all your questions and give you as much information as I possibly can so you can make an educated decision on what you want to do with your mouth. Afterwards, I do complimentary consultations. You can make an appointment. If you have to leave early, you can make an appointment in the back and I'll be happy to examine you at no-charge , to tell you what your options are for whatever type of situation you have. There are people in the audience with teeth missing on the right or the left, full dentures or partials.

Why me? I have a real good friend and he says, what is your reason for existence? Why should they come to you versus anybody else? Why not go to the dentist down the road? Why go to Dr. Gaeta? I'm Board Certified. Board Certification, if you look at it, if your primary care physician is a Board Certified in Internal Medicine, you have to take some extended courses. I have over 1,000 hours of post-graduate education in implant dentistry. I had to take an oral and a written test and had to have 100 cases to meet the criteria you need for you to be able to get board certification.

As a board certified dentist there are fewer than 500 of us, in the world, that are board certified. So just like if you're going to go and see any type of doctor. If you go to a doctor, like my daughter

SammiJo, she broke a bone in her hand, her scaphoid bone. I interviewed her doctor and I think we should all interview our doctors. I asked questions like How many of these types of procedures have you done? What's your success rate? That's what I did for my daughter and rightfully so. We should all interview the doctors we see, after all our lives are in their hands!!!!

I'm trained in both surgical and restoring implants, which means I place the implants and then I put the teeth on top. There are a lot of dentists that don't do both. They say well you need an implant but you need to go see the oral surgeon or Periodontist and then go see doctor so and so and he'll put the implant in. Then you'll come back to me and I will put the tooth on. I do both, all phases of implant dentistry so you don't have to run all over town seeing various doctors.

I am sedation certified. This is the best. I love to sedate people. I am trained in a procedure called parenteral conscious sedation. Do you know what the best sound is that a dentist can hear? The patient snoring!! If you're comfortable that actually adds years to my life. T. I've performed IV sedation since 1988. Your day at the dentist should be like a day at the beach. As we were growing up, it wasn't like a day at the beach.

I'm writing a book and my philosophy of care – I have a passion to serve. This is why I have a passion to serve. I was brought up in Omaha, Nebraska and I was born and raised at working in my parents restaurant "Gaeta's Restaurant"

My parents, Joe and Josephine are here. They're from Omaha, and are down for the winter. This is where I learned how to take care of people, was in Omaha at the restaurant. I'd come home as a dentist and guess what dad would say? Go fill the water and help with the dishes. This is where I learned how to take care of people. I have slides of my family; this is my son, Joey and myself. We did the Disney marathon – half marathon last year. These are two of my four. This is my daughter, Sammi Jo and Joey.

Implants– Josephine, my mother who's in the back has dental implants. I have some patients here that have dental implants. What I would like to do is have them get up and tell you a little about their experience with dental implants.

This is, Herman, who is my surrogate father. He's become a friend and he actually had an upper denture that he doesn't have anymore. He has all fixed teeth. So Herman, do you want to go ahead and tell a little about your experience?

Herman: Sure, I'll be glad to.

One of the best decisions I made in my life, and I made a lot of good ones and a lot of bad ones, was to have implants put into my mouth. The frosting on the cake was I had Dr. Gaeta and his staff do the job. It doesn't matter how long it takes. I had false teeth and I hated them. Most of the time, they were in my pocket. I absolutely hated them. I'd go into restaurants and I would eat with the paper in front of me and do all sorts of crazy things. I'd been looking for implants for years.

I probably got a call from Joe around 10 years ago. There are a lot of pluses. For me, the first time it took a year to do the whole thing. In that process though, I learned a lot about Dr. Gaeta and his staff. I realized that he was dedicated to his profession and he enjoyed his work, which is a big plus. He built a staff around him who were compassionate and caring, so it's been a good experience.

Another plus is that the very first time I went in there, he put me to sleep. He took my false teeth, threw them away and made some temporary teeth. The temporaries were really in a sense almost as good as the permanent ones that I have now. It took a year. First, he put some bone cow bone in there. I was running around saying moo moo. That's what they do to you!! Then it took four or five months for that to get all hooked up and finished.

In the process, I would see Joe and I think I'm part of the family now. I gained a friend with the staff and good Joe. I enjoy coming to see Joe and his staff, even if I'm not going to have any work done. It's been a plus from the very beginning.

Anyhow, after the four months, then he put the implants in and I got a kick out of him. He put them in there and he torqued them. I thought what the heck, are we putting wheels on cars? Whoever heard of getting your teeth torqued? I learned a lot of good things. I recommend that if you're thinking about having anything done, talk with Joe. Go in, see him and think about it. I guarantee it, you will never be sorry that you did and that you picked him and his staff. I'm happy and I'm glad. Like I said, I've become like family and that's a real plus in this world. Thank you.

Dr. Gaeta: The next gentleman is Dave who has a lower denture. I put some dental implants in on the lower denture and with a bar Dave snaps his teeth. Dave, do you want to talk more about your experience?

Dave:

I'm relatively new at this because I only had this done just about two years ago now. My experience with Dr. Gaeta was – this is going to sound funny coming from a patient going to see a dentist– wonderful. A pure pleasure because I had no pain and no discomfort whatsoever afterwards. The process was smooth and like Herman, with the extensive work that I had to have done, it took about a year.

Since I've had it done, I can eat anything I want from steak, peanuts and cashews to apples. I'm not worried about my dentures falling out and embarrassing me if my wife and I are out to dinner.

If you can't eat and chew properly, you don't have good health. If you don't have good health, you don't have anything at all. Being able to eat anything that I want, when I want and knowing that it's doing me good and that my health's good and what it cost me to have the work done was well worth it. In my estimation, you cannot put a price on good health. Like I said before, without it you have nothing.

[Applause]

Dr. Gaeta: Thank you, Dave.

I'd like to introduce you to Loretta Cooper. Loretta's like a surrogate mother to me and she knows if I'm working too hard in the office, she'll tell me. We were talking earlier, it's like she'll grab my ear through the phone when I talk to her. Loretta had partials. She had partial plates that she took in and out. Now she doesn't have partials anymore. We did some implants on Loretta. Loretta, would you like to tell them about your experience, please?

Loretta: Sure. Thank you.

I always like to say its Herman's fault that I'm here, because I watched him go through everything. He's a family friend and I watched him going through the dental implant because I hate dentists. I say it quietly, but I really did. I had terrible experiences as a young person and stayed away from dentists unfortunately, for a lot of years.

I had a lot of damage by the time I saw Dr. Gaeta. I had the partial plates. I had them made when I lived in Pennsylvania. When I came to see Dr. Gaeta, he told me I would leave there that day with teeth in my mouth once he did some of the implants. I was very embarrassed because first, my teeth were being damaged by the plates that I had and I knew that they were wearing out.

I was embarrassed because when I went to a restaurant, I'd always have to get up, walk away, say excuse me, go into the ladies room and take the partials out to rinse them and then put them back in because food particles would get underneath and they would make my mouth very sore.

Dr. Gaeta promised me I wouldn't have that anymore. Like I said, I was petrified and the staff knew I was petrified. They used to literally hold my hand. Dr. Gaeta's brother-in-law isn't here today, that's Mike, but he and I when we sat here we'd go, we are two of the biggest cowards you'd ever see. When I go into Joe and he's going to work on my mouth, he'll make sure I'm very comfortable.

I have work that he's doing now. I had to stop it because I had some surgery and I have two more implants going on this side and God knows what he's going to do over here. I just let him do it now. He tells me what I need and I go okay. Put me to sleep and I don't care what you do! When he puts me to sleep, I really don't care what he does because when I wake up, I'm fine.

Do I have a lot of pain? No. I had been given pain medication. I'm super-sensitive to medications and Joe knows that. The first time he had given me pain medication I couldn't take it and I actually ended up taking Motrin, which was all I needed to get me through was the Motrin. I had one day of uncomfortable-ness, whereas by the next day, the pain was gone.

I walked out of that office. I also had a partial on this side with a tooth, which he took and did away with. I still have bridge work. He's working on that. I was very conscious of my smile. I wouldn't smile. I really was very conscious of my smile because of the clasp and I was afraid of food being there.

He took my partials that day and threw them in the trash and I was like, wow. I came out of there with a temporary and like Herman said the temporaries were just as good. Herman talked about the staff. I can't say enough about the staff. They have been so – they become your children. At my age, they're my children and they really are compassionate. They really care about you. They stayed by me when I got sick one time.

When I'm not there, they pick up the phone and they call to see if I'm okay. So when Herman said it becomes like a family, it really does. The first thing I asked for today was where is Josephine and Joe, because I didn't see them. I didn't know where they were, and they're here today. It was so neat to see them. I'll just say that if you're interested in changing your life – I couldn't eat right either.

If you're interested in changing your life and your smile, I suggest – for me, it wasn't just the smile. It was the eating, which Dr. Gaeta talks about, and I never knew it until I came to the seminars, but I wasn't eating properly. I wasn't chewing properly and today I can go to a restaurant, I can eat what I want, I don't have to be embarrassed and I don't have to run to a restroom to rinse my mouth out.

I also bit him. I always tell this because I did. He said the best thing that happens is when you go to sleep, he hears you snoring. Well, I was snoring so loud one time I guess that I didn't it, but when I woke up I heard Dr. Gaeta saying Loretta, let go of my finger. Loretta, would you open your mouth, let go? I did. I bit him and he still treats me well so that's a plus. That's a good dentist. Thank you.

[Applause]

Josephine (mom):

I come here about every year or so and get dentures and then he put this – what do you call it hanging at the bottom– the implant in and it really helps keep the partials in, so they don't come out. I never have to use any cream, even on the top. He really does good work with my dentures. They're very comfortable. We enjoy coming out here to see him and his family.

He just stays all day and night taking care of the people, making sure they're comfortable. I'm very happy with is work, especially his father whose afraid of the dentist. So he drives for two days to come here and see his son work on his teeth, but I fly. We've been married 57 years, and I've been driving with him for years and

I've got new knees now and I'm going to take the flight.

So my other son is coming back next week to take his dad back home, and I'm going fly back. It's a pleasure being here in Florida. Thank you.

(Video playing)

Diane Sawyer:
Fifteen separate lawsuits have been filed that people have used excessively to say that their denture cream caused them to have difficulty walking, balancing, even devastating nerve damage. Consumer correspondent Elizabeth Levy is here with more.

Elizabeth Levy:
Diane, of those 35 million denture wearers, about one-third use denture cream. Now some of their doctors are saying that excessive use of denture cream has caused health effects so

devastating they can rob you of your independence.

Come on right in here, Ellen. For Ellen Isaacs, it began with a tingling in her toes. Four years later, her balance is gone and simple tasks are not possible. Watch what a challenge it is just to move to the exam table. Then there are the tremors. After multiple rounds of tests, Ellen's neurologist eventually concluded that denture cream was the source of the problem.

Stopping the denture cream use was a key part of her treatment. Ellen says for at least 10 years, she applied Super Poligrip to her dentures once a day and slept in them overnight, but what she didn't know is that the cream contains zinc, which can cause serious illness in high doses.

Ellen:
I would have never equated use of denture cream to what was going

on with my body.

Elizabeth:
Doctor's say too much zinc drives down copper levels in the body. This sets up a chain reaction that affects the spinal cord and makes it hard to walk and maintain balance.

Doctor:
Small amounts of denture cream are certainly safe for people. It's people whose dentures are ill fitting, who are using excessive amounts, who are at risk of running into troubles with toxicity.

Elizabeth:
The authors of a 2008 study in the Journal of Neurology theorized that long-term denture cream overuse was the culprit in the cases of four patients who had unexplained limb weakness and poor balance.

Doctor:

The patients were using at least two tubes of denture cream a week. So, it was longer exposure to very high amounts of denture cream that led to their problem.

Elizabeth:
The FDA does not require that manufacturers list the amount of zinc. So the researchers tested the products themselves. The zinc varied from 17 to 34 milligrams per gram of denture cream. Significant amounts, according to the researchers.

Doctor:
If you have poorly fitting dentures, then seek professional help. Go and see your dentist because we don't want them to be using large amounts of denture cream.

Elizabeth:
The researchers say more study is needed. Denture cream is only considered a Class I medical device by the FDA, so it does not

require a warning label. Just last week, an attorney filed lawsuits on behalf of Ellen and four other denture cream users against two manufacturers. The suits allege the companies failed to warn consumers about the risk.

Attorney:
What we hope to see happen is to actually get a warning label on the product. Unfortunately, there's not the awareness out there and I attribute that in large part to lack of labeling on the product itself.

Elizabeth:
In court, the companies have denied their products are at fault, saying, "There is no scientific proof that denture cream can cause zinc-related illnesses." Glaxo Smith Kline, the company that manufactures Poligrip products, told us "Our product Super Poligrip is safe and effective for daily long-term use when used as directed." Procter &

Gamble, the company that manufactures Fixodent products, said, "All Fixodent products undergo rigorous scientific evaluations and safety testing. All Fixodent products are made, packaged and labeled in accord with FDA manufacturing practices," but Ellen says the companies have a responsibility to the public.

Ellen:
They give you a diagram of how to apply it, but there's no warning. Had there been a warning, I wouldn't be like this.

Elizabeth:
So the key question is how much denture cream should be used?

(End Video)

Dr. Gaeta: With dental implants we can throw away the denture adhesive. Most denture wearers have difficulty chewing these foods. I know some of you have partial plates and some are missing a few teeth. This can be an example, but it doesn't have to be your main course.

I'm going to go over the history of dental implants, and I'm going to talk about frequently asked questions. If anybody has a question, don't hesitate to raise your hand. Dental implants aren't new. Prototypes for current implant design date back to the late 1940's. Long-term implant studies during the past 45 years have given implants a very high rate of success and predictability.

The history of dental implants– Man has been searching for many ways to replace teeth for thousands of years. Attempts were first made at implanting teeth from another person's mouth, which we know never worked. Other materials were tried such as gold, lead, silver and carbon fiber. I was blessed.

I actually purchased a practice in Port Charlotte, Florida from a gentleman who has passed now. His name was Dr. Harold T. Robins. He did his first dental implant the year I was born in 1958. He was a typical dentist. He'd buy and restore things, so he had like a museum in one of the back rooms. He had some carbon implants and none of these old implants worked.

So in 1964, commercially pure titanium was found to be the ideal material for implants. It's the same metal used for hips or knees. This is just a picture of 6,000 A.D., they tried to place oxen bone, I think it was.

What is a modern dental implant?

This is a definition...it's a man-made replacement for the root of a missing tooth. It's an artificial tooth root. So you can take one tooth out and place one implant in. If you have to have dentures, you can throw away your denture, like we did with Herman. We have six to eight implants on top, where we actually fixed the teeth where we cement the teeth, where you don't take them in and out. No plate anymore. I always like to say; giving back the teeth that God gave you.

This is the anatomy, a tooth versus an implant. You can see everything looks the same. The enamel and then the tooth root– nowadays we use screws– before there were sub-periosteal implants, laid implants and those different types of implants are around still, but the profession has leaned more towards titanium screw. This is just an x-ray of an implant placed.

Why do they work?

There's a term called Osseointegration, which is the biological attachment of a metallic implant to vital bone. Bone loves titanium. Together, bone and titanium form a firm anchor. An anchor is what makes an implant one of the best options for replacement today.

What happens is when you place the screw with threads the bone grows and locks the threads. You have to wait a certain length of time. Osseointegrated dental implants, so you can do a bridge if you're missing some teeth and then place some crowns on top of those. That's one option.

They're made in a large variety of sizes, shapes accommodating nearly every situation. In the early days – this is a manufacture thing. My implants are better than these implants and nowadays they all work. All the dental implants out there work. So, if you come in and say what kind of implants do you use? I use what's called a, Bio Horizon implant system.

It has a square thread because there's a lot of research and development behind the implant design and the surface here and if there are any engineers in the room, stress equals force. So the more surface area you have on the implant design, plus stress. So there's a lot of research and development behind all the different implants. This is just a plethora of all the different implant designs.

In the old days, they had cylinders that didn't have any threads on them. That's what my mother has, but there are no threads on the implant. I placed my mother's implants 12 years ago.

The advantages of dental implants, is no more food restrictions. If you have an upper denture, you could throw it away, place implants and be able to chew anything. They're stable and comfortable. They don't move. A lower denture moves a quarter of an inch, even the best fitting one. They're easy to maintain and you treat them like natural teeth.

So, if you have dentures or replacement implants, you come back to the dentist and you see Donna, our hygienist and she helps you maintain those implants because you can form plaque around them, just like a regular tooth. You could develop bone loss as well. They don't decay, so there are no root canals and they are considered a long-term solution. Implants also maintain facial bone size and height. The implants stop bone resorption.

Implants maintain bone size and bone height, so if you lose teeth, the bone in that area will shrink. I have a model that I'm going to pass around, if you're missing a couple of teeth in an area, you'll notice that there's less bone in that area. This is a schematic of what happens, as you can see you constantly lose bone. Once you take teeth out, you continuously loose bone in the area where the teeth were removed for the rest of your life.

Without teeth, the bone in your jaw begins to shrink it's called 'bone resorption' and it can be very dramatic. You could wear dentures to maintain your facial form, but the denture wearer does not arrest the bone shrinkage. Nothing arrests the bone shrinking, so it constantly gets worse, unless you place dental implants.

Once you place implants, it stops the bone loss because your body thinks it's a tooth. When you stimulate the bone, just like if you put a cast on an arm or a leg, if you take the cast off after six to eight weeks, it looks smaller. That's because of lack of use. The muscles actually got smaller because of lack of use and also the bone shrinks due to lack of stimulation.

The amount of bone loss in the first year after tooth removal is much greater than the following years, so you lose maybe about four millimeters of bone per year. Then after the first year, the bone loss on the lower arch resorbs faster than the upper arch.

Once you take them out, if you have periodontal disease, if your teeth are bad and you have to do something, you've been to a dentist and he says, we've treated your periodontal disease, now you want to shrink the pockets and eliminate the periodontal disease. You'll have a lot of bone loss and you're leaning towards implants, if they're all bad, you can take them out. I perform that procedure. I can use IV sedation. and take them all out at once ,you won't remember a thing!! We can put the implants in at the same time, provided you have enough bone. Actually, I can put a temporary bridge on also, if the condition of the bone is adequate, so you never go without teeth.

There are different situations.

This is what can happen to your face. The jaw – your chin gets closer to your nose over time. Teeth support the lower one-third of the face. Here's an interesting long-term study by Harvard that patients who maintain most or all of their natural teeth or have missing teeth replaced by fixed bridge work or have teeth supported by dental implants live 9.8 years longer than those patients who have lost all their teeth . So it's about quality of life, and adding years to your life...

We talk about the "golden years". You retire, you move to Florida and what do you do? Well, let's go to dinner, like Loretta was talking about. I had a patient one time, she said when I go to the restaurant and I open the menu, I'm looking at the menu and I'm saying to myself, I can't eat this. I can't chew this. I can't chew this. Then she relied on pastas or the things that don't require a lot of chewing. That's why I have these types of seminars because I like for people to have the quality of life that they deserve. Placing dental implants to anchor your dentures so you can chew again!!

So, you retire, you worked hard and I call it the 'just get by syndrome' too. A lot of seniors "just get by." I can chew okay. But how good can you really chew?

When you lose you teeth, you lose bone and bone needs stimulation to maintain form, density and strength. Tooth loss causes movement of adjacent or opposing teeth. So if you lose a couple of teeth, the other teeth fall into that space so the space has to be maintained. The lower jaw protrudes out farther than the upper jaw. So as the chin gets closer to the nose, the lower jaw goes out. Your lips thin, especially the upper lip. Sagging of the muscles contributes to the jowls or a witch's chin appearance. It looks like it sticks out and it decreases the overall height of the face.

With teeth present, your jawbone height is about from one to one and half inches and then over time; it continually shrinks and continually gets worse. This is just another example of approximately four millimeters of bone loss per year. This is an x-ray where they show a lot of bone here and then over time you lose bone. Loss of bone height is significant reason for placing implants as soon as possible because it stops the bone loss!

> Why don't the dentures fit as well as when you got them?

It's because of bone loss. You're

constantly losing bone. It's due to lack of retention because once you take your teeth out, your jawbone has a lot of surface area for the dentures to stay in. Over time, it just shrinks and becomes shallow. This is another example of bone loss. So don't let it happen to you! And The condition continually gets worse!

This is an x-ray. You can see this is where the nerve is. This is where the mandibular nerve is over time. Then as after 25 years you experience extreme bone loss.

. A lot of times what happens is this mandibular nerve will end up on top of the mandible, so when you bite down it will hurt in this specific area. That's because the metal nerve as it's called, ends up on top of the jawbone. You can maintain your bone mass with dental implants and eliminate this problem from happening.

Bite force deteriorates steadily

with dentures. This is significant. Your average bite force with molars and natural teeth is 150 to 250 psi, which means pounds per square inch, which is a unit of measuring force. The maximum bite force for a denture wearer is less than 50 psi . So as soon as you have your teeth out, your bite force goes to 25% of what it was with natural teeth. Even if you have two teeth left, and they are in bad shape. You go to to the dentist and he takes one of them out, and then he decides the last tooth has to be removed . You're going, oh now what?

Therefore, as soon as you take those two teeth out, the denture flops around considerably. So even though you have one and a half teeth or one tooth left, it still stabilizes the lower denture . As soon as you have those teeth taken out, all the sudden you can't chew! Patients wearing dentures for more than 15 years have a maximum bite force of only 5.6 psi.

Another example of a situation I've experienced is when I use the articulating paper we call it, like carbon paper and have a denture wearer, who has had dentures for 15 years. I told her to bite down. She bit down, I said bite real hard and she bit down. Her head was shaking trying to squeeze her teeth together I pulled the paper out!!!, She had no bite force to chew anything.

Then there's a progression of problems. You can't chew or masticate food, you start getting indigestion, the doctor gives you the purple pill to take and all the antacids and your life expectancy slows like we talked about.

Once you place the dental implants, your bite force can increase up to 85% and your bite force can even increase up to 300%, so you can actually gain your bite force back, dramatically improve the chewing function and bite force retention and stability.

Health consequences of poorly performing dentures cause significant reduction in chewing performance and lower consumption of fruits and vegetables because they're so hard to eat. Then you get like I said the gastrointestinal disorders. You get stomach problems because you can't masticate your food properly, you can't chew your food. You've got to be able to chew your food. It's important.

I've had gastroenterologists send me letters and say she needs to be able to chew better. Her inability to masticate her food is making her malnourished. You can't swallow. What are they doing now? They're stretching the esophagus. Has anybody heard of that?

Better taste with implants.

Bridges in place often cover and obstruct the palette, which plays a major role in your sensation of taste. So denture wearers, we could eliminate the palette and snap the denture in and have some of your olfactory or taste senses back.

Again, the palate is uncovered, allowing you to taste and enjoy your food, as you should. It's a big quality of life issue. Ask yourself can this affect my life expectancy? Absolutely! As we discussed earlier, it's yes, people feel their social life is affected. I've had patients tell me that they don't want to go out to eat with certain people because they'd be embarrassed.

Some people can't wear both dentures all the time. Some people can only wear the top. They can't wear the bottoms. Most denture wearers have problems with their bottom dentures.

Difficulty with speech– there's constant discomfort. Always a sore somewhere, you maybe just get by. You avoid certain foods. Don't eat in public. Some people don't eat in public and as we mentioned, dentures can compromise your health.

So everybody says well, can I have implants? Am I a candidate for implants? Yes. Everyone is a candidate. If you don't have the bone, we can grow the bone. What's that mean? Where do you get the bone? You can buy the bone, you can take the bone from the mineral synthesis or the tibia anything is possible.

I did it on my mom and that has a real high success rate. The bone is safe. Perfectly safe. It has a high success rate. It's been around for a long time. So it all comes back to quality of life like I said. Age is not a factor. I've placed implants on 9-year olds, 95, 90, 96 was probably the oldest. You have to be in reasonably good health. If you're on medication or if you're on a blood thinner, we have to stop the blood thinner for a period.

I always consult with your doctor. I do a lot of conscious sedation. I do a lot of IV. It's like twilight sleeping. If you've ever had a colonoscopy or a minor surgical procedure, you had a lot of that, but I touch base with the doctor.

This is what we're going be doing. Any complications, if we have to do a sinus lift, I will send you for a CAT scan. Actually, I have a mobile CAT scan. You can come to the office and take a CAT scan for a diagnosis. The CT scan helps with diagnosis to make sure there's nothing in the sinus and shows me how much bone you have, where the bone is and then you can move the implant around with your mouse and put the implant in there at any angulation that you need and it's a wonderful treatment.

You have to be committed to good oral hygiene. It's an investment, so you have to keep them clean and you have to come in every three months, and we have a hygienist look at you and make sure you're cleaning them properly.

Frequently asked questions– How long does it take? There's a series of steps. Treatment varies depending on the patient's needs. It varies from one implant to full mouth implants and it provides immediate use.

For the lower anterior, it takes anywhere from two to five months so, from zero to two and a half months. If you have a lower denture and it's moving around, your upper feels pretty good and you just want to concentrate on the bottom, what we can do is place the implants in and sometimes – it all depends on how dense your bone is. So if you put it in and it's tight to a certain number, then we can put the bar on and put the teeth on right away. Just like if you're missing one or two teeth.

It all depends on how dense the bone is. Your anterior mandible, down here is like oak so it's dense and doesn't take as long for the implants to integrate, for the bone to grow and lock with it; two and a half months.

Then the posterior, which is your bottom jaw in the back. It's not as dense as the lower anterior, so it takes a little longer back here. Then the maxillary anterior, which is the front, takes a little bit longer. Then posterior maxilla, which is the back upper right, upper left. If you're missing a tooth, that's more like pine or sometimes balsa wood. So you have to wait longer – four to 12 months, like we did with Herman. Sometimes it takes a year, but the nice thing about it is that it works. So it is a process.

Here's a big question.

> Do you ever have to go without teeth?

Never! I never send you out of the office without teeth, because we all have busy lives and it's not very appetizing for me either, if you go and smile at the grocery store and they say where are your teeth?

Has anybody ever heard of this concept teeth in a day? With teeth in a day, it's possible. Just like with Herman, if you take your teeth out and you have enough dense bone, you can place the implants in and then put some teeth on it right away. So, it all depends on the situation and the individual, but that's possible. So it depends on the individual case and the bone quality and mass.

Success rate like I said, in dental

implants has been shown to be 98-100% successful. They have the highest success rate.

Does it hurt, Herman?

Herman: No. Even the temporaries felt natural and I don't even think about them. I've just got natural teeth today. I'm going on about 10 years. I'm 87 years old, so either myself or my teeth should start to deteriorate.

Dr. Gaeta: There's always some of this stuff.

Modern dental techniques allow dental implant procedures to be an outpatient service with minor post-operative discomfort. The key is within any type of surgery, anybody can place them in, what you're feeling is that the bone has no nerve endings, so when you place the implant in the, there are no nerve endings. The gums have the nerve endings.

So it's all in the tissue design when you do your surgery. What I've learned over the years is it's your gums; it's how you manipulate the gums and how Atraumatic you are with that type of procedure. Some dentists are better than others. Some dentists have better hands than others. Some dentists have more training than others.

It's just like with a doctor, if you have a cardiologist who's going to do open heart or whatever and you ask, how many have you done? When was the last time you did one? Do you do them often? How many have you done this year?

Guest: Is there any rejection?

Dr. Gaeta: Yes, sometimes that can happen, but luckily by the grace of God, I've had probably 1% failure.

Guest: What can you do then?

Dr. Gaeta: You take it out, you place more
              bone and then you place another
              implant.

Guest: Can they break off?

Dr. Gaeta: No, they usually don't break
              because of the design of the
              implant. They have a hex inside
              and because of the strength they
              usually don't break. In earlier
              days with the old designs they
              would have snapped off right at
              the tumble, but they don't break.

ABOUT THE AUTHOR

Dr. Joseph Gaeta Jr. is a full-blood Italian (Sicilian third-generation). He grew up in Omaha, Nebraska, where, growing up, he worked in his parents' restaurant. It was at Gaeta's restaurant that Joseph Gaeta learned how to work hard, how to multi-task, how to work with his hands, and how to serve.

He was put to work cooking at the ripe old age of six. Dr. Gaeta recalls standing on a milk crate helping make garlic bread. Here he not only acquired excellent eye-hand coordination and multi-tasking skill, but also the value of hard work. Even after becoming a dentist and owning his own business, a return home to Omaha and to Gaeta's meant Papa Gaeta would put the doctor to work filling water glasses and waiting tables.

During the 70s and 80s, Gaeta's catered to

large parties of 300 and 400 people. The whole family worked together to make these a success. This is where Dr. Gaeta first learned about serving and taking care of people. As he says, "life is about service." Dr. Gaeta graduated from Creighton University, School of Dental Science, in Omaha. In 1989, he moved to Sarasota, Florida where he opened his practice. Through the years, he has logged over 1,500 hours in post-graduate dental implant education and has been placing dental implants for over 20 years.

In 2000, Dr. Gaeta achieved Board Certification status with the American Board of Oral Implantology/Implant Dentistry (ABOI/ID). He is also a Diplomat of the ICOI and an associate fellow of the AAID. Fewer than 500 dentists worldwide have achieved such status. Dr. Gaeta is trained in both surgical and restorative Implant Dentistry. There are few dentists in the United States who do both.

Additionally, he is certified in IV conscious sedation. By definition, parenteral conscious sedation means the patient responds to verbal stimulation but remembers very little, or nothing at all, about the procedure. The patient loses all track of time and the doctor can perform up to five times the amount of dental work. This is "absolute Heaven" for the patient and the doctor. Dr. Gaeta says the best sound a dentist can here is the patient *snoring*! This process, as the doctor says, makes going to the dentist feel like a "day at the beach." And why shouldn't a day at the dentist be like a day at the beach?

Dr. Gaeta has a relentless passion to serve and help others. One of his passions is to leave a legacy that lasts beyond his lifetime. For this reason, he has founded the World Dental Implant Awareness Organization (www.WDIAO.ORG), whose mission is to create awareness in the world about the benefits of dental implants for people who suffer from tooth loss. As a devotee of health and fitness, Dr. Gaeta is also a tri-athlete and marathon runner. In the Walt Disney Goofy Challenge, he and his son, Joey, run the Walt Disney World Half Marathon together on Saturday, then, on Sunday, Dr. Gaeta runs a full Marathon. It is called the Goofy Challenge because you have to be *goofy* to do both. Dr. Gaeta believes in "a sound mind in a sound body." The temple we have been given by our Creator needs to be nurtured through diet and exercise to be of maximum efficiency to serve.

For more information on Dr. Gaeta and his products and coaching programs please visit:

www.DrJoeGaeta.com